TOP SCORE

WORKBOOK 3

JAMES STYRING

OXFORD

UNIVERSITY PRESS

OXFORD
UNIVERSITY PRESS

Great Clarendon Street, Oxford OX2 6DP

Oxford University Press is a department of the University of Oxford.
It furthers the University's objective of excellence in research, scholarship,
and education by publishing worldwide in

Oxford New York

Auckland Cape Town Dar es Salaam Hong Kong Karachi
Kuala Lumpur Madrid Melbourne Mexico City Nairobi
New Delhi Shanghai Taipei Toronto

With offices in

Argentina Austria Brazil Chile Czech Republic France Greece
Guatemala Hungary Italy Japan Poland Portugal Singapore
South Korea Switzerland Thailand Turkey Ukraine Vietnam

OXFORD and OXFORD ENGLISH are registered trade marks of
Oxford University Press in the UK and in certain other countries

ISBN: 978 0 19 412909 1

Printed in China

ACKNOWLEDGEMENTS

*The Publishers would like to thank the following for their kind permission to reproduce
photographs and other copyright material*:
Alamy pp17 (Bubbles Photolibrary / boy working in shop), 21 (Rune
Hellestad / Mourhino), 23 (mountain biker), 26 (hockey), 28 (Inuits), 35 (f1
online / solar panels, bio-diesel), 42 (Phototake Inc. / tired girl), 50 (Robert
Rayworth / Kefalonia), 53, 54 (Digital Archive Japan / rubber tyres), 65 (Giles
Robberts / motorbike in China); Corbis pp 4 (Niall Benvie / landscape), 5
(Yann Artus-Bertand / crocodile), 7 (Jeffrey L Rottman / sharkcage), 13 (Patrik
Giardino / school students), 14 (John Henley / woman), 29 (© Royalty Free /
teenagers), 30 (© Royalty Free / mobile phone), 33 (Paul Hardy / chewing
gum), 51 (You Sung-Ho / Reuters / Woo-Suk Hwang and Snuppy), 53 (MIT
Media Lab / epa / MIT laptop), 54 (Stacy Morrison / fabric, J Berndes / A.B. /
zefa / concrete, Carrott Productions / zefa / plastic, © Royalty Free / scissors,
shoes, David Zimmerman / glass of water, H.D. Thoreau / wood), 55 (David
Seawell / robotic machine), 59 (Rebecca Cook / Michael Sessions), 60 (Rainer
Holz / zefa / boy and moped), 63 (Jeff Christensen / Boorman and McGregor),
66 (Richard Cohen / moped), 70 (John Todd / rugby scrum), 71 (Mark Garten
/ man proposing), 72 (Darryl Bush / Schwarzenegger, Seoul National
University / Handout / Reuters / Snuppy); EMPICS / AP p 19 (Sebastian John /
Delhi Marathon); Getty Images pp 3 (Don Bonsey / girl wearing sunglasses),
10, 25 (Howard Kingsnorth / mirror imaging), 28 (Bongarts / Berlin
Marathon), 35 (Lester Lefkowitz / wind turbines), 52 (Grant Taylor /
Hollywood sign), 57 (AFP / Martin Halstead), 72 (AFP / Martin Halstead);
Fotolia p. 48; OUP pp. 6 (all), 38.

Illustrations by: Javier Joaquin / The Organisation pp 6, 8, 16, 20, 31, 36, 43,
45, 49, 58, 69; Oliver Hutton p. 41 (map)

Getting started

Vocabulary

Character adjectives

1 Complete the crossword. Find the secret word.

1 'He doesn't like meeting new people.' 'Is he s_____?'
2 'She's always happy!' 'I know. She's really c_____.'
3 'Sorry, I can't lend you £5.' 'Huh! You're so m_____.'
4 'This situation is very s_____.' 'Yes, it's ridiculous!'
5 'Don't be rude to them.' 'Why? Are they especially s_____?'
6 'You should be more positive. You're so m_____ sometimes.'
7 'I get up at eleven on Saturdays.' 'That's really l_____!'
8 'My mum gave me £20!' 'Wow, she's g_____.'

```
          ¹S  H  Y
      ²□  □  □  □
   ³□  □  □  □
          ⁴□  □  □  □
   ⁵□  □  □  □
⁶□  □  □  □  □
          ⁷□  □  □  □
   ⁸□  □  □  □
```

Phrasal verbs

2 Match the verbs 1–6 with the particles a–f.

1 give   [f]
2 look   [ ]
3 put   [ ]
4 shut   [ ]
5 take   [ ]
6 turn   [ ]

a after
b down
c off
d on
e over
f up

3 Complete the sentences with the phrasal verbs from exercise 2.

I had to *put on* my sunglasses, it was so sunny.
1 My dad is going to _____ smoking next month.
2 I always _____ my little sister on Saturdays.
3 This is boring. Let's _____ to BBC3.
4 Remember to _____ your computer every night.
5 Don't _____ your jacket. It's cold.

Sports

4 Find and write the sports words.

s t a m c i n g s y   *gymnastics*
1 r a t a k e   _____
2 c l i n c g y   _____
3 d r o w i n b a s n o g   _____
4 m o t i n b a n d   _____
5 a b b a l l s e k t   _____
6 l o l a l e l b v y   _____

5 Complete the text with the sports words from exercise 4.

At British schools, students often play team sports, such as *basketball* and (1) _____. Racket sports, such as (2) _____, are also very popular. Students often do (3) _____ and (4) _____ in the school sports hall. (5) _____ is a winter sport, and not many students can afford it. Most of the students have bikes and in their free time they go (6) _____.

The natural world

6 Find eight words in the wordsquare.

F	O	R	E	S	T	D	R	O	E	N	W	H
B	M	O	U	N	T	A	I	N	C	A	O	I
O	H	C	P	S	I	G	V	N	A	E	D	L
E	A	K	M	E	S	B	E	A	C	H	A	F
S	T	R	E	A	M	I	R	I	O	V	E	N

-ed and *-ing* adjectives

7 Choose the correct adjectives from the box to complete the sentences.

> amazed amazing bored ~~boring~~ embarrassed
> embarrassing interested interesting tired
> tiring

Don't watch that film. It's *boring*.

1 'Are you OK?' 'No! I went to bed at 2 a.m. and I'm _____!
2 My cousin's got lots of new channels on digital TV. It's _____!
3 Playing sports every day is quite _____.
4 I forgot my friend's birthday last week. I felt so _____!
5 This new magazine is really _____.

do, *have*, *make* and *get*

8 Complete the dialogues with *do*, *have*, *make* or *get*.

'Did you *do* your maths homework?'
'Yes! I always *do* my homework!'

1 'Call me when you _____ home.'
   'OK, but I have to _____ the washing up first.'
2 'I didn't _____ your letter.'
   'I'm sorry. Sometimes we _____ mistakes.'
3 'Do you _____ pocket money every month?'
   'Only if I _____ my bed every day.'
4 'Why do your grandparents _____ a rest every afternoon?'
   'They're old and they _____ very tired.'

Consolidation

9 Complete the crossword with words for objects in the house.

Down ↓
1 I don't have to do the washing up. We've got a d_____.
2 You write words on a computer with a k_____.
4 You keep your shirts and dresses in a w_____.

Across →
3 A f_____ keeps food cold.
5 A c_____ heats food.
6 You click and select things with a m_____.
7 My books are on the s_____ above my bed.

Grammar

Present simple or present continuous?

1 Complete the blog with the present simple or present continuous form of the verbs in brackets.

> It 's raining, so I _____ (**1** sit) at home with my baby sister, Emma.
> I _____ (**2** think) about what to write in my new blog!
> _____ (**3** you / listen) to music while you read my blog?
> I _____ (**4** listen) to the new Linkin Park CD. _____ (**5** you / have got) it? It's amazing! Have you heard it?
> Emma _____ (**6** not listen) because she _____ (**7** sleep), as usual. She isn't a Linkin Park fan. She _____ (**8** not like) any of my music! In fact, _____ (**9** babies / like) music? I _____ (**10** not think) Emma does. I'm going to stop blogging now. I'm going to do my homework.

2 Write present simple or present continuous questions.

you / listen to / me / ?
Are you listening to me?
No, I'm sorry. Can you repeat that?

1 you / speak / English / ?

_____

Yes, we learn it at school.

2 they / do / their / homework / ?

_____

Yes, they're at home now.

3 what / she / say / ?

_____

Your music is too loud!

4 he / play / the guitar / ?

_____

Only at the weekends.

Past simple or past continuous?

3 Complete the sentences with the words in the box.

> ~~did you see~~   didn't call   didn't hear   fell over
> got   was going   was playing   watched
> were studying   were they doing

Did you see the match last night?

1 'Where were you at eight o'clock?'
   'I _____ to school.'
2 He _____ while he _____ football.
3 I _____ you because it was very late.
4 'What _____ at two o'clock?'
   'They _____ biology.'
5 I shouted your name again and again, but you _____ .
6 We _____ home at six and we _____ TV.

4 Complete the text with the correct form of the verbs in brackets.

Some National Geographic scientists *were driving* (drive) across a desert in Niger, Africa, when they _____ (**1** notice) an unusual bone. They _____ (**2** stop) their Land Rover and _____ (**3** start) to look for more bones. After three days, the leader, Paul Sereno, _____ (**4** see) a very big bone.
Another scientist _____ (**5** work) a few metres away, so he _____ (**6** help) Sereno. They _____ (**7** find) the head of a crocodile, but not an ordinary crocodile. It was a 'super-crocodile', with a head two metres long. Its body was probably about thirteen metres long – as big as a bus. It _____ (**8** live) 110 million years ago and it probably _____ (**9** eat) dinosaurs. They _____ (**10** call) it the 'super-croc'.

5 Look at the picture and correct the sentences.

Dad was listening to the radio.
He wasn't listening to the radio.
He was cooking.

1 Tina was watching TV.
   She _____
   _____

2 Mum was writing an email.
   She _____
   _____

3 Sam was going to school.
   He _____
   _____

Comparatives and superlatives

6 Write comparative sentences with *than* or superlative sentences.

saltwater crocodile / large / crocodile / today
The saltwater crocodile is the largest
crocodile today.
It / small / a super-croc
It is smaller than a super-croc.

1 a bus / tall / a person
   _____

2 the cheetah / fast / animal
   _____

3 a cat / slow / a cheetah
   _____

4 the monkey / intelligent / animal
   _____

7 Look at the information. Are the sentences true or false? Explain your answers with comparative adjectives, superlative adjectives or *as ... as*.

Daniel Watson	
cheerful ★★★★★	good at maths ★★★★
hard-working ★★★★	serious ★★★
intelligent ★★★★	tall ★★★★
good at swimming ★★★★★	

Emma Taylor	
cheerful ★	good at maths ★★★★★
hard-working ★★★★★	serious ★★★★★
intelligent ★★★★★	tall ★★
good at swimming ★	

Alex Brown	
cheerful ★★★	good at maths ★★
hard-working ★★	serious ★★
intelligent ★★	tall ★★★★★
good at swimming ★	

Daniel Watson is the tallest.
False. Daniel is not as tall as Alex
Brown. Alex is taller than Daniel Watson
and Emma Taylor.
Daniel is more serious than Alex.
True, but Daniel is not as serious as
Emma. Emma is the most serious.

1 Alex is the best at swimming.
   _____
   _____

2 Daniel is better at maths than Alex.
   _____
   _____

3 Alex is not as intelligent as Daniel.
   _____
   _____

4 Emma is more cheerful than Alex.
   _____
   _____

5 Alex is not as hard-working as Daniel.
   _____
   _____

Reading

Shark tourism kills surfers

Surfers have made the headlines again with their recent claim. Shark attacks on humans, they say, are increasing because of the tourism industry. *Dorothy Cotton* **reports from Cape Town, South Africa.**

A [5] For twenty years, there have been few shark attacks in South African waters – until now. This year there have been five attacks, two of them fatal.

B [ ] Mark Turner (32) of Llandudno Beach, near Cape Town, suffered a terrifying attack last month. 'We were waiting for a wave about 200 metres from the beach,' explains Mr Turner. 'Suddenly, something hard hit my legs. I saw a huge dark shape moving under the waves. Then it pulled me under the water. The force was astonishing.''It took me a few seconds to realise that it was a shark. I hit it on the nose and it went away. Then it came back and bit my surfboard! My mate put me on his surfboard and swam with me back to the beach.'

C [ ] Mark had had an exhausting but extraordinary escape. He had injuries on his legs and feet, but he was lucky to be alive. Not everyone is so lucky.

D [ ] Attacks by great white and tiger sharks have always been fairly common in the USA and Australia. But what is causing the rise in attacks in South Africa?

Surfers blame the problem on shark tourism. Boats take tourists to areas where there are a lot of sharks. The tour operators throw small fish into the water to attract the sharks. Then the tourists go diving. But it is not as dangerous as it sounds: they watch the sharks from the safety of a large metal cage.

E [ ] Surfers say that sharks have begun to associate human activity with food, and that is why more sharks are attacking humans.

---

1 **Read the text. Match the headings 1–6 with the spaces A–E. There is one heading that you do not need.**

1 Lucky getaway
2 A surfer's story
3 Stop feeding sharks
4 Race to save lives
5 Shark attacks increase
6 Why more attacks?

2 **Answer the questions. Use full sentences.**

What is causing more shark attacks, according to surfers?

Tourism is causing more shark attacks.

1 How is the number of shark attacks in South Africa changing?

_____

2 Where was Mark Turner when a shark attacked him?

_____

3 How did he make the shark go away?

_____

4 How did Mark Turner's friend save him?

_____
_____

5 Is shark tourism dangerous for tourists? Why?

_____

6 Why are there more shark attacks?

_____
_____

Grammar

Present perfect

1 Complete the text with the present perfect forms of the verbs in brackets.

| Home | Results | Fixtures | FA Cup |

Not United!

It *hasn't been* (not be) a very good season yet for Nottingham United. 'What _____ (**1** go) wrong?' asks Fiona Stringfellow.

Some of their problems are due to the injuries that players _____ (**2** have) since August. They _____ (**3** substitute) the goalkeeper twice and star striker Liam Chandley _____ (**4** not score) since his accident in Oxford.

So, _____ United _____ (**5** give up)? United's manager, Peter Bright, says not. Although they _____ (**6** not start) the season well, he remains optimistic about their game against Derby City this Saturday.

2 Complete the sentences with the words in the box.

> already ~~before~~ ever for just never
> since yet

I can't swim. I haven't had swimming lessons *before*.

1 Our school team is very good. We've _____ lost a game!
2 Have they revised for the test _____?
3 We've lived here _____ 1999.
4 Have you _____ been to Africa?
5 She was at home two minutes ago. I've _____ spoken to her.
6 Has he been in the team _____ a long time?
7 I've _____ met him. I've known him for years.

3 Rewrite the sentences using *already* or *yet*.

Hasn't she finished her homework?
Hasn't she finished her homework yet?

1 They've bought a laptop.
_____

2 Wait. Mum hasn't drunk her coffee.
_____

3 Have you read my magazine? That was quick!
_____

4 We've been to London so we're going to York.
_____

5 I've told you the answer.
_____

6 She hasn't visited the UK.
_____

4 Write sentences with *just*.

It *has just started* to rain.

1 The cyclists _____ (fall off) their bikes.
2 One cyclist _____ (hurt) his leg.
3 The woman _____ (open) her umbrella.
4 The boy _____ (take) a photo.

⑤ Write sentences and questions with the present perfect and *for*, *since*, *ever* or *never*.

he / play / badminton
He has never played badminton.

1 Julia Ward / run / a marathon ?

_____

2 they / study / French

_____

3 she / be / at the doctor's / 10 a.m. / ?

_____

4 he / not do / his homework / two weeks

_____
_____

5 I / not break / my leg / I was eight years old

_____
_____

6 you / visit / Paris / ?

_____

7 I / have / this watch / 2002

_____

8 we / play / squash / three years

_____

Present perfect or past simple?

⑥ Complete the questions with the words in the box.

ago ask before did did did do go has ~~have~~
heard in met play speak ~~seen~~ when win

Have you seen my brother?

1 Could you _____ English two years
_____?
2 _____ you _____ your
homework last night?
3 Did you _____ horse-riding
_____ you were ten?
4 _____ she _____ the new
CD?
5 Why _____ Ciara _____ you
that question yesterday?
6 Have you _____ her parents _____?
7 _____ they _____ tennis this morning?
8 Did Juventus _____ the championship
_____ 2005?

⑦ Correct the mistakes in each sentence.

I just read that book. Didn't you read it yet?
*I have just read that book. Haven't you
read it yet?*

1 We've met her last week. She been fascinating.

_____

2 I never spoke to her before. Did you?

_____

3 They've left at five o'clock. They didn't got home yet.

_____

4 We didn't watch this DVD yet. Has you saw it?

_____

Consolidation

**⑧ Complete the interview with the past simple
or present perfect form of the verbs in brackets.**

ABC Tell us about your job.
MSF I'm a doctor and I work for DWB – that's
Doctors Without Borders.
ABC How long *have you been* (you / be)
interested in medicine?
MSF Well, I _____ (1 be)
very interested in medicine since I
_____ (2 be) a young girl.
My parents were farmers, and I
_____ (3 not learn) about
medicine until I was at university.
ABC When _____
(4 you / start) at DWB?
MSF I _____ (5 start) when
I was 29, so I _____
(6 work) for MSF for four years.
ABC What _____ (7 be) the
best thing about working for DWB?
MSF The best thing is also the worst thing.
I _____ (8 meet) a lot of
fascinating people but the work
_____ (9 not be) easy.
Our patients usually feel very sick before
they find a doctor. I remember Mutuze, a
tiny, thin baby. She had a very bad
stomach-ache and a temperature.
We _____ (10 be) very
worried about her but she got better.

Communication

Vocabulary Extreme adjectives

1 Complete the sentences with the words in the box.

> ~~astonishing~~ exhausting fantastic fascinating
> freezing terrifying tiny

That's astonishing. I can't believe that you can speak six languages!

1 London is cold in February. In fact, it's often _____.

2 Skiing is really _____. I'm so tired!

3 'My sister's getting married.' 'That's _____ news!'

4 We never watch horror films. My mum finds them too _____.

5 He loves insects. He finds them _____.

6 My baby brother is _____. I've never seen such a small baby.

Parts of the body

2 Label the parts of the body.

1	toes	6	_____	11	_____
2	_____	7	_____	12	_____
3	_____	8	_____	13	_____
4	_____	9	_____	14	_____
5	_____	10	_____		

3 Complete the sentences with parts of the body.

Your wrist connects your arm and your hand.

1 A hand has four _____ and one _____.

2 Your _____ is inside your neck.

3 Your _____ connects your leg and your foot.

4 The forehead and cheek form part of your _____.

Extension STAYING HEALTHY

4 Match 1–5 with a–e to make short dialogues.

1 'How do you avoid getting a sore throat in winter?' [b]

2 'Why do footballers touch their toes?' [ ]

3 'I need to take more exercise.' [ ]

4 'What are you doing?' [ ]

5 'I've just done fifty press-ups!' [ ]

a 'I'm doing yoga. It helps me to relax.'

b 'I take vitamins, but I don't take other medicines.'

c 'That's enough. Have a rest for ten minutes now.'

d 'To stretch their thigh muscles before they play.'

e 'Well, why don't you go jogging or cycling?

Speaking At the doctor's

5 Complete the dialogue with the words in the box.

> 've fallen over ~~has happened~~ have ... hurt
> hurts shouldn't go 've sprained stretch take

Doctor   What has happened, then?

Tom   I (1) _____, doctor.

Doctor   (2) _____ you _____ yourself?

Tom   Well, my finger (3) _____.

Doctor   Let me look at it. Hmm. Yes, you (4) _____ it. Don't (5) _____ the finger and (6) _____ some aspirin.

Tom   Yes, doctor. Thank you. Perhaps I (7) _____ to school?

Doctor   No, no, Maz. It isn't that serious!

Writing

An informal letter

1 **Match the expressions 1–5 with the spaces A–E in the letter.**

1 I hope to hear from you soon
2 Dear
3 Sorry I haven't written for ages
4 Lots of love
5 Thanks for your letter

(A) [2] Sally

How are you? **(B)** [   ], but **(1)** I haven't felt great. Guess why not? **I've fallen off my skateboard!**

I **(2)** _____ **broken my right arm in three places** and **sprained my wrist**.
I **(3)** _____ at home now, but I was in hospital for **four days last week**.

I feel **(4)** _____ better now.
In fact, I **(5)** _____, having
(6) _____ good time! I can **watch TV and relax** all day!
My sister (7) _____ writing this letter for me. Have you noticed that her handwriting **(8)** _____ the same as mine?

(C) [   ]. It was great. I always love reading your news.
Anyway, **(D)** [   ].
Write soon.

(E) [   ],
Tina

Informal language

2 **Choose the correct informal language from the box to complete spaces 1–8 in the letter.**

> 'm 'm 's 've a dead am am
> an extremely have have not ~~haven't~~
> is is not isn't loads very much

3 **Write an informal letter.**

- Think of an illness or accident. Make notes.
- Change the **bold** words in the model in exercise 1.

_____
_____
_____
_____
_____
_____
_____
_____
_____
_____
_____
_____
_____
_____
_____
_____
_____
_____
_____
_____
_____
_____
_____
_____
_____

Quick check

Vocabulary

1 **Write the extreme adjectives.**

1 cold   f_____   4 interesting f_____
2 good   f_____   5 surprising a_____
3 small   t_____   6 tiring   e_____

2 **Write the word that connects the parts of the body.**

1 ankle / foot / knee / thigh   _____
2 cheek / chin / eye / forehead   _____
3 hand / elbow / finger / wrist   _____
4 back / chest / stomach / waist   _____

3 **Complete the sentences about staying healthy.**

1 'T_____ this medicine and
  h_____ a good rest,' said the doctor.
2 She can only d_____ five press-ups, but
  she can t_____ her toes easily.
3 I don't want to g_____ cycling. I'm
  going to h_____ a rest.

Vocabulary review

4 **Complete the dialogues with the words in the box.**

> doing fingers freezing huge keyboard
> legs look into plug in put on terrifying

Tony   Did you (1) _____ the problem
         with Sandra's computer?
Charlie I started, but I can't (2) _____
         the (3) _____. I broke three
         (4) _____ on Friday while I
         was (5) _____ karate.
Tony   Oh, no! OK. I can help you, but first I'm
         going to (6) _____ my jacket.
         It's (7) _____ in here!

Sandra   I didn't realise that great white sharks
         were so (8) _____. Diving with
         them sounds (9) _____!
Louise   No, really, it's fantastic! But keep your
         (10) _____ in the cage!

Grammar

5 **Write present perfect affirmative and negative sentences with *for*, *since*, *ever* or *never*.**

1 we / see / her / yesterday ✗
  _____

2 you / eat / shark meat ?
  _____

3 it / be / sunny / a week ✓
  _____

4 they / drive / a car ✗
  _____

6 **Complete the dialogue with the past simple or present perfect form of the verbs in brackets.**

Cycle+   Now for our readers' questions. Phil
         asks:
         _____ (1 you ever / hurt)
         yourself cycling?
Andy   Oh, yes! I _____ (2 crash)
         more times than I can remember.
Cycle+   Really?
Andy   Oh, yes. I _____ (3 break)
         that leg, this arm, these three fingers …
Cycle+   When _____ (4 you / have)
         your most recent accident?
Andy   Er, I _____ (5 fall off)
         my bike yesterday, but I
         _____ (6 not hurt)
         myself, luckily.
Cycle+   Good! And now for another question …

Grammar review

7 **Choose the correct answer.**

1 It hasn't rained **for / since** three weeks.
2 We **'ve watched / watched** the match yesterday.
3 Have you ever seen this film **yet / before**?
4 They **haven't finished / didn't finish** yet.
5 We haven't spoken to them **just / yet**.
6 Tim is **oldest / older** than Charlie.
7 **Did you play / Have you played** tennis on Friday?
8 I've **ever / never** played rugby.
9 I **was waking up / woke up** at 11 a.m. yesterday.
10 She's **already / yet** finished that book.

Reading

Summerhill School

Most schools have a fixed timetable and school rules. The curriculum is compulsory and students have to attend every class. But a few schools have a different system.

A [5] Summerhill School is private, so parents pay to send their children. It is also a boarding school, which means that the students sleep there during term-time. But what makes Summerhill very unusual is that it is democratic.

B [ ] The teachers do not write the school rules at democratic schools. Instead, everyone at the school has an equal opportunity to make the rules. At Summerhill, there are three big meetings every week. Students and teachers propose rules and everyone votes to accept or not accept each rule. Every term, they normally have between 150 and 230 rules!

C [ ] Yes. For example, one meeting voted to allow students to go to bed at any time of night. However, after a few noisy students accidentally woke up others who were sleeping, another meeting voted to bring back bed times. Democracy works because the students have to live with the rules that they have made.

D [ ] Yes. Students can choose any subjects from the normal primary or secondary school curriculum. Classes are not obligatory, and although some students do not attend classes for a while, eventually they want to do something more interesting than play football. It is very motivating for students to choose which courses to do. Summerhill offers GCSE exams, but most students do their 'A' levels at other colleges.

E [ ] Summerhill opened in 1921, and it is the oldest democratic school in the UK, but it is not the only one. In fact, there are at least 70 more around the world.

F [ ] Parents say that Summerhill students are tolerant, honest and generous. They are good at discussing and negotiating, and they are also good at making decisions. This is because of their participation in the democratic process. Summerhill students leave school with good 'life skills' and they usually do well at university.

1 **Read the text quickly. When did Summerhill School open?**

_____

2 **Match the questions 1–6 with the spaces A–F.**

1 Do democratic schools really work?
2 Do the students learn anything?
3 Is Summerhill the only democratic school?
4 What does 'democratic' mean?
5 What kind of school is Summerhill?
6 Why do parents choose Summerhill?

3 **Answer the questions. Use full sentences.**

What is different about a boarding school?
Students sleep there during term-time.

1 Who makes the rules at Summerhill?

_____

2 Why is the democratic system effective?

_____

3 Why do many students choose to go to lessons?

_____

4 Why are Summerhill students well prepared for life?

_____

_____

Grammar

Modal verbs
Obligation and necessity

1 Complete the dialogue with the words in the box.

> don't have to wear   has to have
> ~~isn't allowed to sit~~   must remember
> must continue   mustn't arrive   mustn't chew
> Is … allowed to see   Is … allowed to wear

Mrs Palmer I'm Sara Palmer's mother. How is she doing?

Teacher Well, Sara isn't allowed to sit next to her best friend at the moment and her marks are much better as a result.

Mrs Palmer (1) _____ she _____ her friends at lunchtime?

Teacher Yes, she is, but her classroom behaviour (2) _____ to improve. Then she can sit with her friends in class. Also, Sara (3) _____ to bring her books with her every day and she (4) _____ late.

Mrs Palmer Tell me. (5) ___ she _____ anything that she likes at school, even jeans? I was very surprised when Sara told me. Is it true?

Teacher Hmmm, well, although students (6) _____ a uniform, the rule is no jeans. Also, she (7) _____ neat hair – no more dreadlocks, please. And of course, chewing gum is prohibited, so Sara (8) _____ gum at school.

2 Write negative sentences or questions using the correct form of *have to*, *must* or *be allowed to*.

> you / have to / do / homework every evening ?
> *Do you have to do homework every evening?*

1 she / have to / finish / her project tonight ✗

_____

2 we / must / cheat / in exams ✗

_____

3 we / have to / do / sports ?

_____

4 they / allowed to / ride mopeds ?

_____

5 we / allowed to / use / mobiles in class ✗

_____

6 you / must / copy / your homework ✗

_____

7 my little sister / allowed to / wear make-up ✗

_____

8 Paul / have to / resit / the maths exam ?

_____

3 Correct the mistakes in each sentence.

> I be allowed watch TV until midnight.
> *I'm allowed to watch TV until midnight.*

1 He musts listens to the teacher.

_____

2 Does he has to doing homework tonight?

_____

3 We are must to revise for the exam.

_____

4 You're allowed go home early?

_____

5 They not must arrives late.

_____

6 Do have we play sport?

_____

7 She not allowed wear jewellery.

_____

8 You haven't must to chew gum.

_____

4 Match 1–5 with a–e. Then complete a–e with the correct form of the verbs in boxes A and B.

A   ~~be allowed to~~   be allowed to   not have to
must   mustn't

B   arrive   do   have   listen to   ~~wear~~

1   Those earrings look really nice! | e |
2   Put your MP3 player in your bag! | |
3   You're late again! | |
4   But I don't want a haircut, Mum. | |
5   Some classes are voluntary. | |
a   We _____ long hair at our school!
b   You _____ music in lessons.
c   We _____ art or music.
d   You _____ before 8.30 a.m. every day.
e   *Are* you *allowed to wear* them at school?

Modal verbs
Possibility and certainty

5 Complete the sentences with *can't*, *might* or *must*.

It's difficult to see, but it *might* be him.
1   This _____ be my book. Mine is in better condition.
2   It _____ be hot outside. It's very sunny.
3   It's snowing. It _____ be cold outside.
4   This huge T-shirt _____ be hers. She's tiny!
5   We _____ go to Italy, but we haven't decided.

6 Rewrite the sentences using the verbs in brackets.

I'm sure this isn't the right book. (can't)
This *can't be the right book.*
1   It's possible that we'll pass the exam. (may)
We _____
2   Perhaps you'll find the book in the library. (might)
You _____
3   I'm certain that it's midday now. (must)
It _____
4   Maybe you'll get top marks. (could)
You _____

Consolidation

7 Complete the dialogue with the words in the box.

're allowed to do   aren't allowed to walk
can't be   could wait   don't have to go
don't have to return   ~~have to be~~
may be   must go

PC Bill   Hello, hello, hello. What are you lads doing here, then? You *have to be* at school from Monday to Friday.
You **(1)** _____ around the streets, you know.

Graeme   Yes, officer, but we **(2)** _____ _____ to school today.

PC Bill   I **(3)** _____ old, but I know that today's Friday! You **(4)** _____ to school every schoolday, boys. It's the law.

Neil   But our school isn't open this week. We **(5)** _____ until next Tuesday. It's our holidays and we **(6)** _____ anything that we want.

PC Bill   That's enough! I'm taking you back to school … [*five minutes later*] … and here we are. But the school is closed! It **(7)** _____ true!

Graeme   Yes, officer. We **(8)** _____ here, but it's a long time until Tuesday!

Communication

Vocabulary Education

1 Complete the text with the words in the box.

> curriculum degree GCSEs ~~primary school~~
> secondary school timetable

My youngest brother is ten and he goes to the
primary school in Regent's Road. My brother and I
go to the same (1) _____. I love
school and I enjoy every subject on the
(2) _____ except science. My
brother and I start school at the same time because
we have the same (3) _____.
We're sitting our (4) _____ at the
moment and my eldest brother has just finished his
'A' levels. He's going to do a (5) _____
at university next year.

2 Match the verbs with the nouns in the box.
There are some words that you need twice.

> a degree an exam high marks

      fail *an exam*   3 pass _____
1 get _____   4 resit _____
2 get _____   5 sit _____

Compound nouns

3 Label the pictures with compound nouns.

1 *tap water*

4 _____

2 _____

5 _____

6 _____

3 _____

Extension compound nouns

4 Read the definitions. Find the words.

this goes under your plates, bowls and glasses
(e t a l o h l b t o)
tablecloth

1 cleans dirty clothes (s w a g n i h   c h e a m i n)
   _____

2 eyewear for sunny days (g a s s u n l e s s)
   _____

3 your contacts' details are in this
   (d r e s a d s   k o b o)
   _____

4 a bicycle with an engine (k o b i r m o t e)
   _____

5 a sofa for one person (c r a m h a i r)
   _____

6 cleaning at home (s h o r e k o w u)
   _____

Speaking Giving advice (1)

5 Complete the dialogue with the suggestions in
the box.

> OK, you might have to cycle, then.
> You should go by bus.
> Well, why don't you go by car?
> How about walking?

Annie Look at the time! I have to be at basketball
practice by ten. What shall I do?
Ben (1) _____
Annie I can't. There isn't one until 10.15.
Ben (2) _____
You could ask your mum.
Annie No, I can't. My parents are at work.
Ben (3) _____
Annie Don't be stupid! I have to be there by ten.
It's too far.
Ben Yes, but it's good for you.
(4) _____
Annie Yes, that's a good idea. It only takes ten
minutes.

Writing

An email

1 **Look at the email and answer the questions.**

1 Who wrote it? _____

2 Who is it to? _____

2 **Complete the email with the words in the box.**

> You should ask   You must be   you mustn't be
> Why don't you look   you shouldn't wear

dear cousin ajay

how are you uncle mehta said that you wanted to work in a shop so heres some advice

(1) _____ at the job adverts in your local shops

the most important thing is that (2) _____ _____ late you have to wear smart clothes but (3) _____ your school clothes

i put the food on the shelves and i also help customers thats the most interesting part of the job but its also the most difficult (4) _____ very careful with money

im not allowed to eat while im working i have to wait until my breaks (5) _____ before you eat or drink things from the shop

i love earning my own money i hope you enjoy it too

see you soon

amit

Punctuation

3 **Read the email slowly and think about the questions. Then write the complete email, using the correct punctuation.**

- How should each sentence start?
- Where and how should each sentence end?
- Read each sentence. What other punctuation do you need to add?

_____
_____
_____
_____
_____
_____
_____
_____
_____
_____
_____
_____
_____
_____
_____
_____
_____
_____
_____
_____
_____
_____
_____
_____
_____
_____
_____
_____

Vocabulary

1 Complete the text with the correct form of the education verbs in the box. There are some verbs that you do not need.

> approve fail get pass present remake
> resit sit suspend

Dear Duncan

You were right. Maria has (1) _____ her last exam and she's already got the results. And yes, she's (2) _____ all her GCSEs! She always (3) _____ really good marks. She hasn't (4) _____ an exam since she arrived at this school. I'm the opposite. I have to (5) _____ about half of my exams!

See you soon,

Abdullah

2 Read the descriptions. Write the compound nouns.

1 You can send text messages with this.
   m_____ _____
2 You use this after you have a shower.
   h_____
3 You clean your teeth with this.
   t_____
4 This wakes you up every morning.
   a_____ _____

Vocabulary review: Units 1–2

3 Complete the sentences with the words in the box.

> computer cut degree fantastic finger games
> secondary tap tin water

1 Don't _____ your _____ on the _____ -opener.
2 My laptop _____ is _____! I can play computer _____ on the train.
3 Excuse me. Is it _____ water in that _____ jug?
4 She did 'A' levels at Mill Hill _____ school, and then she got a _____ from York University.

Grammar

4 Complete the sentences with the correct form of *have to*, *must* or *be allowed to*. There is usually more than one answer.

1 We _____ study maths. It's compulsory.
2 _____ you _____ wear a uniform?
3 Students _____ talk during lessons.
4 _____ you _____ take phones to your school?
5 We _____ arrive on time for school.

5 Complete the sentences with *can't*, *could* or *must*.

1 Her face went white. She _____ hate insects.
2 It _____ be midnight already! It only feels like ten thirty.
3 It's snowing. You _____ be freezing!
4 I'm not sure. We _____ have a tin-opener at home.

Grammar review: Units 1–2

6 Read the text and choose the correct answers.

Schools in England and Wales

School (**1**) **has been** / **was** compulsory between the ages of five and sixteen (**2**) **for** / **since** 1972. Children (**3**) **might** / **have to** attend primary school between the ages of five and eleven (Years 1–6) and they then go to secondary school.

Three years later, when they begin Year 10, the students (**4**) **mustn't** / **are allowed to** choose some subjects, but the compulsory subjects that students (**5**) **may** / **must** study include English, maths, science, information and communication technology (ICT), physical education (PE), and citizenship.

There are other optional subjects which students (**6**) **don't have to** / **mustn't** study. With foreign languages, schools (**7**) **must** / **mustn't** teach one or more languages from the European Union, but in some schools, the students (**8**) **may** / **mustn't** also study Chinese, for example. Some students (**9**) **might** / **must** prefer history, geography or art.

Students (**10**) **might** / **have to** stay at secondary school until Year 11 and then they take their GCSEs.

3 A sporting life

Reading

Go, Budhia, go!

A Every day, Budhia Singh and his coach take a bus from Puri to Bhubaneswar, in eastern India. Then Budhia runs all of the 58 km back to Puri. Budhia's coach, Biranchi Das, follows Budhia on a bicycle. It takes Budhia seven hours to complete his run, not including a break in the middle when he sleeps.

B A lot of people can run long distances. What makes this Indian boy's story astonishing is that he is just four years old. 'I want to see Budhia's name in *The Guinness Book of Records* as the youngest person in the world who has run a marathon,' says Biranchi.

C When he is older, Budhia wants to run in international competitions. 'I want to win an Olympic medal for India,' says Budhia.

D Biranchi Das is the coach at a local sports club. One day, Budhia was being a bully to other boys at the club. Mr Das was angry and said to Budhia, 'Run around the track until I say "Stop".' Budhia started running and Das went out. When he came back five hours later, Das had forgotten about Budhia and was amazed that he was still running. 'Has he just started running again?' he asked the other boys. But the boys said 'No'. Budhia had refused to stop running until Mr Das said 'Stop'.

E 'Budhia wasn't tired or thirsty after he had run for five hours,' explained Mr Das. He realised that Budhia had special talents and he offered to train him.

F Budhia took up the offer immediately. He was born in a poor area, and he had only eaten a small amount of rice every day, but now Mr Das gives him meat, eggs and fruit as well. Budhia has become a local celebrity, but he does not care about his fans. 'I just want to become a great runner and win races', he says.

1 Read the text quickly. What is special about Budhia Singh? _____

2 Are the sentences true or false? Explain your answers.

Every day, Budhia Singh runs from Puri to Bhubaneswar.
False. He takes a bus to Bhubaneswar and then he runs back to Puri.

1 Biranchi Das cycles 116 km every day.

_____

2 Budhia cannot run for seven hours non-stop.

_____

3 Budhia needed a drink after he had run for five hours.

_____

4 Budhia is famous in Puri.

_____

3 Answer the questions. Use full sentences.

Why is Budhia's story surprising?
His story is surprising because he is only four years old.

1 What does Budhia want to do for his country?

_____

2 How long did Budhia run around the track?

_____

3 Why was Budhia's diet not very good?

_____

4 How has his diet improved since he started running?

_____

Grammar

Past perfect

1 **Match 1–7 with a–g to make sentences.**

1 After she'd collected her prize `c`
2 We couldn't get into the stadium ☐
3 Schumacher won three races ☐
4 The team were astonished ☐
5 I got really wet ☐
6 The penalty was easy because ☐
7 After they'd played in France ☐

a after he'd changed to the new car.
b because I'd forgotten to bring my jacket.
c she waved to her fans.
d the goalkeeper had jumped too early.
e because we'd lost our tickets.
f they played a few games in Italy.
g because they hadn't expected to win.

2 **Complete the text with the verbs in the box.**

> ~~had been~~ had died hadn't eaten hadn't had
> Had you run had run had sent hadn't thought

Before he met Biranchi Das, Budhia Singh's life
had been very different. Budhia
(1) _____ big meals until he met Mr Das.
Budhia's father **(2)** _____ before Budhia
was three, and his mother
(3) _____ enough money to feed all her
children. She
(4) _____ Budhia to work for Mr Das at
the sports club.

Mr Das was very impressed that Budhia
(5) _____ around the track hundreds of
times.

'**(6)** _____ a lot before you met Mr Das?'

'No! I **(7)** _____ about it! We didn't have
time for things like that. But now I really want to be
a runner.'

3 **Read the sentences. Which action happened first? Number the pictures 1 and 2.**

A 2   B 1

She was late for the exam because she hadn't heard
her alarm clock.

A ☐   B ☐

1 When Jon woke up, Terry had gone out.

A ☐   B ☐

2 When he didn't stop at the red light, he failed his
motorbike test.

A ☐   B ☐

3 She sat down after they had painted the seat.

A ☐   B ☐

4 He had problems with his teacher because sheep
had blocked the road.

4 Complete the sentences with the past simple or past perfect form of the verbs in the box.

> become fall get up have not go move
> ~~play~~ study watch

Had you *played* tennis when you took up badminton?

1 Why _____ you _____ home after school had finished?

2 Did you call her after you _____ that film?

3 We'd finished all our homework before we _____ dinner.

4 Where had they lived before they _____ here?

5 I was in a hurry because I _____ late.

6 _____ she _____ French before she visited Paris?

7 I'd met Keira Knightley three years before she _____ famous.

8 Jimmy _____ asleep before he finished the book.

5 Rewrite the sentences using *because* and the past perfect.

> I read the results on the internet. I knew the score.
> *I knew the score because I'd read the results on the internet.*

1 I didn't have her phone number. She didn't send it to me.

_____

_____

2 They were hungry. They didn't eat anything for lunch.

_____

_____

3 He lost his bus ticket. He had to walk home.

_____

_____

4 Her hair was wet. Her hairdryer broke.

_____

_____

5 I didn't pass the test. I didn't revise.

_____

_____

Consolidation

6 Complete the text with the past simple or past perfect form of the verbs in brackets.

José Mourinho is one of the best football club managers in the world. Here are a few questions from a Chelsea FC fan website.

Chelsea Football Club
Visitors' frequently asked questions

Had **Mourinho** *played* **football before he** _____ **(1 become) a manager?**

Yes. Although he was not very successful as a footballer, Mourinho had developed a reputation as a brilliant manager when he _____ (**2 work**) at Portuguese clubs in the 1990s.

He _____ (**3 manage**) FC Porto of Portugal for two years before he _____ (**4 join**) Chelsea in 2004.

Had the club been successful before Mourinho arrived?

Yes, Chelsea _____ (**5 have**) great success with manager Claudio Ranieri, and Chelsea's performance _____ (**6 continue**) under Mourinho. He _____ (**7 sign**) Ricardo Carvalho and Paulo Ferreira, two players who _____ (**8 play**) in his team at Porto. He also signed Didier Drogba, who _____ (**9 be**) at Marseille before.

Has Mourinho's personality been a problem?

He is argumentative, but this has only caused problems occasionally. For example, in 2005, a referee sent Mourinho off the pitch after he _____ (**10 argue**) with Liverpool fans.

Communication

Vocabulary Sport

1 Match 1–5 with a–e to make sentences.

1 He took part in [d]   a the girls' athletics team.
2 Juventus beat [ ]   b the women's Giro d'Italia.
3 We've taken up [ ]   c Chelsea 3–0.
4 She's training [ ]   d the 200m race.
5 Somarriba won [ ]   e badminton.

2 Complete the text with the words in the box.

> athlete ~~coach~~ competition fans races
> spectators team train win

A good coach must spend a lot of time training her
(1) _____ . Each (2) _____ has to
(3) _____ hard every day. This keeps them
in top condition and it means that they win their
(4) _____ . On race days, the team's
(5) _____ can make a lot of difference,
too. They can create an exciting atmosphere and
they can help a team to (6) _____ .
Sometimes, when there aren't many
(7) _____ in the stadium, the
(8) _____ isn't as exciting.

Personality adjectives

3 Substitute the adjectives with a synonym.

Sportspeople are usually ~~energetic~~ active.
1 She's famous for being ~~fearless~~ d_____ .
2 Don't be ~~anxious~~ n_____ . You'll win!
3 Luckily she's ~~decisive~~ q_____-
   _____ .
4 Snowboarding is not for the ~~cautious~~
   u_____ .
5 They asked him because he's so ~~reliable~~
   t_____ .
6 My mum's ~~relaxed~~ e_____-_____
   about my new hobby, scuba-diving.

Extension ANTONYMS

4 Find the opposites of the adjectives.

> ~~active~~ decisive kind loyal reliable
> secure thoughtful

H	U	N	R	E	L	I	A	B	L	E	K	F
I	N	D	E	C	I	S	I	V	E	I	N	A
U	K	T	H	O	U	G	H	T	L	E	S	S
Y	I	N	A	C	T	I	V	E	N	O	N	U
I	N	S	E	C	U	R	E	U	R	O	J	S
L	D	I	S	L	O	Y	A	L	R	E	S	S

5 Complete the sentences with adjectives from the wordsquare in exercise 4.

It's unkind to say bad things about people.
1 She's _____ . She never knows what to do.
2 He never thinks about other people. He's very
   _____ .
3 My best friend is never _____ .
4 They're always late. They're so _____ .

Speaking Making arrangements

6 Complete the dialogue with the words in the box.

> ~~do you fancy~~ go on let's meet that depends
> what are you doing when is it

Bill Do you fancy taking part in a cycling race?
Ben (1) _____ . I don't like
       competitions.
Bill Oh, (2) _____! Don't be
       so unadventurous.
Ben Oh, OK then. (3) _____ ?
Bill It's in two weeks time, but we need to train
       first. (4) _____ this
       weekend?
Ben I'm busy on Saturday, but not on Sunday.
Bill (5) _____ at my house at
       ten o'clock.
Ben Sure. See you on Sunday.

Writing

A description of a sport

1 Complete paragraphs a and b with the words in the boxes.

> ~~don't need~~ cycle need to learn practise
> should train

a

> You *don't need* a coach to learn mountain biking, but
> you (1) _____ first. Start in a local park
> or at a track. (2) _____ how to steer and
> stop. You also (3) _____ how to fall off
> your bike safely. For fitness, (4) _____
> for an hour without stopping.

> find go practise take

b

> (5) _____ cycling 30 km regularly.
> Then (6) _____ into the countryside
> with a few friends. (7) _____ your own
> off-road routes. When you are experienced,
> (8) _____ lunch and go for the whole
> day.

Organising ideas

2 Read the paragraphs, including a and b from exercise 1. Match paragraphs a–f with the functions 1–6 to organise the text.

1 introduction ___f___
2 background ☐
3 advice about how to take up the sport ☐
4 further information ☐
5 information about equipment ☐
6 conclusion ☐

c

> Cycling has been a popular sport for many years. Since
> 1996, mountain biking has been an Olympic sport, too.
> Millions of people use them to get to work or school,
> and for fun, but I never knew that bicycles had only
> existed for 120 years.

d

> Mountain bikes are specially made for cycling
> off-road. They can cost anything from £70 to £7,000!
> You need a helmet and a pair of gloves.

e

> Are you fit and energetic? Then try mountain biking!
> But remember, this is not a sport for the
> unadventurous. Go on – go mountain biking!

f

> Mountain biking combines a feeling of freedom with
> the thrill of speed. It is exhausting as well as great fun.

3 Read the text in the correct order.

Vocabulary

1 Complete the dialogue with the sports words in the box.

> beat coach race spectators take part in
> take up train win

Gina We're going to (1) _____ the inter-schools cross-country (2) _____ next weekend.

Laura Are you going to (3) _____? Who's your (4) _____?

Gina We don't need one! Every year we (5) _____ Silver Street School.

Laura Will there be many (6) _____?

Gina Yes. Cheney Boys' School team are going.

Laura Really? I'm going to (7) _____ running! Can I (8) _____ with you?

2 Choose the correct answer.

1 **Disloyal / Reliable** people are never late.
2 Sportspeople have **active / easy-going** lives.
3 Divers are quite **daring / trustworthy**.
4 It's **kind / decisive** to give presents.
5 Be **anxious / cautious** when you go out at night.
6 Footballers need to be **thoughtful / quick-thinking**.

Vocabulary review: Units 1–3

3 Complete the dialogues with the words in the box.

> clock cut failed headache pass resit
> terrible

Polly I feel (1) _____. I've got an awful (2) _____.

Sue And you've got a huge (3) _____ on your forehead. That must hurt!

Dan Did you (4) _____ your exam?

Lee No, I (5) _____ it. I was late because I didn't hear my alarm (6) _____.

Dan Oh well, you can (7) _____ it in September.

Grammar

4 Complete the sentences with the past perfect or past simple form of the verbs in the box.

> arrive go not have lose not play twist
> walk watch

1 Had he read the book before he _____ the film?
2 We _____ lunch when the phone rang.
3 Had the plane left when you _____ at the airport?
4 I had a sore throat because I _____ for a walk in the rain.
5 They _____ home after they had missed the bus.
6 Had he run a long way before he _____ his ankle?
7 She _____ tennis because she hadn't brought her racket.
8 I couldn't open the tin because I _____ the tin-opener.

Grammar review: Units 1–3

5 Complete the text with the words in the box.

> are not allowed to discovered had cheated
> had taken had not run have ever run have to

The marathon has been the most important race (1) _____ the first modern Olympic Games in 1896. Runners (2) _____ train very hard to run the 42.2 km of a marathon course. And for most runners, the marathon is the longest race that they (3) _____.

Obviously, the most basic rule is that you must (4) _____ the whole marathon. You (5) _____ catch a bus, for example. The fastest runners (6) _____ finish a marathon in just over two hours, but for most people any time under three hours is good.

But for 33 runners in the Berlin Marathon in 2000, the race was shorter. Why? Because they (7) _____ the underground! The organisers quickly (8) _____ that the runners (9) _____ the whole race. The electronic chips on the runners showed where and when they (10) _____.

Revision: Units 1-3

Vocabulary

1 **Match the adjectives 1–6 with the extreme adjectives a–f.**

1 cold ☐
2 exciting ☐
3 frightening ☐
4 interesting ☐
5 surprising ☐
6 tiring ☐

a astonishing
b exhausting
c fascinating
d freezing
e terrifying
f thrilling

2 **Complete the text with words for parts of the body.**

Human bodies are symmetrical. On each hand, we have a (1) t_____ and four (2) f_____. Similarly, each leg has a (3) t_____ at the top, then a (4) k_____, an (5) a_____ and a (6) f_____. And at the end of each leg, both of our (7) f_____ have five (8) t_____.

3 **Choose the correct answer.**

1 Did you **fail** / **suspend** all your GCSEs?
2 I need to **approve** / **pass** the biology test.
3 I haven't got high **marks** / **notes** this term.
4 I don't want to **present** / **sit** another exam.

4 **Complete the compound nouns.**

1 h _ _ rd _ _ er
2 _ oo _ _ _ _ _ sh
3 _ _ _ -o _ _ n _ _
4 _ _ ke- _ _ b _ _
5 _ _ ter _ _ g
6 al _ _ _ _ _ _ ck

5 **Complete the text with the sports words in the box.**

anxious   beat   coaches   easy-going   fans
teams   train   win

When football players (1) _____ with the (2) _____ during the week, they're usually quite relaxed. Even on a match night, the players seem (3) _____.
But for the football (4) _____, it's a different experience. They're always very (5) _____ that they might lose. They dream that their club will (6) _____ all the other (7) _____ and that they will (8) _____ the league.

6 **Complete the dialogue with the words in the box.**

athletes   body   degree   exhausting   marks
nervous   pass   timetables   train

Dan (1) _____ who are also studying for a university (2) _____ can find it hard to get good (3) _____ and (4) _____ their exams.

Liz Is that because they feel (5) _____?

Dan Well, yes, but that's the same for everyone. No, the biggest problem is with their (6) _____. They have to go to all the same classes as the other students and write the same number of essays, but sportspeople have to (7) _____ for several hours every day as well.

Liz Their training must be (8) _____, too. Studying can't be easy when your (9) _____ is very tired.

Grammar

1 Write present perfect sentences and questions.

1 you / ever / break / your leg?

_____

2 my sister / not get / a degree / yet

_____

3 they / win / every game / for / two years

_____

4 we / read / that book / already

_____

5 I / not fail / an exam / since / I was ten

_____

6 he / just / take up / tennis?

_____

7 she / not do / this sport before

_____

8 you / hurt / your knee again?

_____

2 Complete the sentences with the present perfect form of the verbs in brackets and the words in the box.

already ever for just since yet

1 '_____ he _____
_____ (visit) you in the holidays?'
'Yes, he _____ _____
_____ (be) here twice. The second time
was last July.'

2 We _____ _____ (not live) in
that house _____ I was ten.

3 '_____ you _____ (finish)
reading that email _____?'
'Yes, I _____ _____
_____ (read) it. I finished it a minute
ago.'

4 I _____ _____ (not be) at
this school _____ very long.

3 Complete the dialogue with the present perfect or past simple form of the verbs in brackets.

Andrew _____
(1 you / take up) a sport yet?

Peter Yes. I _____ (2 be) in the
hockey team since the beginning of
term. You obviously _____
(3 not read) the emails I sent, have you?

Andrew Sorry. I _____ (4 not have)
much time this term. So, what's it like?

Peter Actually, I'm really enjoying it and the
other day we _____ (5 play) our
first match!

Andrew Wow! _____ (6 you / win)?

Peter Er, no. I _____ (7 score) a goal.

Andrew Well done!

Peter No! It was for the other team. The ball
_____ (8 go) into our net!

4 Write sentences with the correct form of *be allowed to, have to* or *must*. There is sometimes more than one answer.

1 Smoking is prohibited.
We _____ smoke.

2 It is necessary to do homework every day.
We _____ do homework
every day.

3 Can you come home after midnight?
_____ you _____
come home after midnight?

4 Uniforms are obligatory.
We _____ wear uniforms.

5 Mobile phones are prohibited.
We _____ use mobile phones.

6 Sometimes they play sports, but it isn't necessary.
They _____ play sports.

5 Complete the sentences with the verbs in the box. There is more than one answer.

can't could might may must

1 Don't be silly! It's dark outside – it _____ be three p.m.
2 I can hear voices. They _____ be here somewhere.
3 He failed last year, but I think he _____ pass this year.
4 No one else in the team has the key. Anna _____ have it.
5 The shop _____ be open. I'm not sure.
6 That _____ be right! Yesterday there was £100. Now there's only £30.

6 Write affirmative and negative sentences and questions in the past simple and the past perfect.

1 how many exams / you / fail / before / the teacher / call / your father?

_____

_____

2 we / not win / many matches / when / play / against Manchester

_____

_____

3 where / they / go / after / they / see / Jim's band?

_____

_____

4 he / feel / terrible / because / he / play football in the rain

_____

_____

7 Rewrite the sentences using *because* and the past perfect.

1 I didn't train. I lost the race.

_____

2 We arrived first. We took an earlier bus.

_____

_____

3 My sister failed her exams. She didn't study enough.

_____

_____

8 Complete the dialogue with the past simple or past perfect form of the verbs in brackets.

Carol I saw you at school today. What was the problem?
Mark I _____ (1 not pass) the science test.
Carol Well, you often fail tests!
Mark But I _____ (2 not be) at school, so I _____ (3 not know) the answers.
Carol Why hadn't you been at school?
Mark I was ill. I _____ (4 stay) at home because I _____ (5 not feel) well for a few days.
Carol Did the science teacher know that you _____ (6 be) ill?
Mark Yes, but she _____ (7 not be) sympathetic!
Carol Hmmm … I'm not surprised! You probably failed because you _____ (8 not pay) enough attention all term!

9 Complete the text with the words in the box.

did … catch did not escape had not gone
might find picked up had raced
had not reached have arrested must be walked

Italy's unluckiest criminal

Police in Rome (1) _____ the unluckiest criminal in Italy.

Luciano Rossi is a thief. He went to Rome airport because he thought that he (2) _____ some bags with expensive things in them.

Mr Rossi waited in the Arrivals hall and watched. Soon, a group of Americans (3) _____ into Arrivals. 'They (4) _____ rich,' Mr Rossi thought, so he (5) _____ a bag and he ran.

But the victim was very quick-thinking. Maurice Greene immediately chased the thief. Mr Rossi (6) _____ the exit before Mr Greene caught him.

So, how (7) _____ Mr Greene _____ him?

Well, the Americans (8) _____ here as tourists. They were members of the USA athletics team and they were in Rome for the World Athletics Championships. It is not surprising that Mr Rossi (9) _____ because he (10) _____ against the fastest runner in the world.

Culture focus

1 Do the culture quiz. Look for the answers in your Student's Book and Workbook if necessary.

Section A   Find and write the nationality.
(1 point for each correct answer)

1 Who first celebrated Mardi Gras?

The _____

2 What nationality are Fitch and Maloney, the bobsleigh heroes?

_____

3 What nationality were the first European settlers in North America?

_____

4 What nationality is the four-year-old marathon runner?

_____

5 Who celebrates Columbus Day on the second Monday in October?

The _____s.

6 Which people live in Greenland?

The _____.

CAMAIREN   MAJANACI

TUINI   DANINI

CRENFH   DLANGEN

Section B Answer the questions.
(3 points for each correct answer)

1 How many colonies of North America signed the Declaration of Independence?

_____

2 In which two countries is home schooling prohibited?

_____

3 Name one subject on your curriculum which British students do not have to study.

_____

4 Where did kayaking start?

_____

5 How many British children under the age of sixteen have a part-time job?

_____

6 How did a group of runners cheat in the 2000 Berlin Marathon?

_____

7 What does David Beckham wear every match?

_____

8 Which English football club did manager José Mourinho join in 2004?

_____

Your score?   / 30

4 | Communication

Reading

The language of hope

Ĉu vi parolas Esperanton? – 'Do you speak Esperanto?'
No? Then you should probably reply, *Mi ne komprenas vin.* – 'I don't understand you.'

What language is this?
It is called Esperanto.

Where does Esperanto originate?
Ludovic Zamenhof invented Esperanto in 1887. The name 'Esperanto' comes from *D-ro Esperanto* ('Dr Hopeful'), which was Zamenhof's new name in Esperanto.

Why did Zamenhof invent Esperanto?
Zamenhof wanted to create a language that people could use in international contexts. He did not intend Esperanto to replace native languages such as English or Spanish. He thought that Esperanto could be a second language instead of languages such as English, Spanish or French.

Zamenhof believed that Esperanto might create a stronger sense of international community and understanding.

Did Esperanto become the international language?
No. English is the world's second language – for the moment. Only 380,000,000 people speak English as a first language, but 2,000,000,000 people can speak some English. However, Mandarin Chinese is the world's biggest first language, with 900,000,000 native speakers.

Up to 2,000,000 people speak Esperanto fluently, and there are more than 100 magazines in Esperanto. As many as 2,000 people speak Esperanto as their first language, but few believe that it will become a universal second language.

Do people still learn and speak Esperanto?
Yes. Although Esperanto is not an official language anywhere, it is part of the national curriculum in China, Hungary and Bulgaria. Esperanto is very easy to learn; after one year, students can communicate easily with other Esperantists. According to some linguists, learning Esperanto also makes it easier to learn other languages afterwards. Are you tempted to try Esperanto instead of English?

Ĝis la revido! – 'Goodbye!'

---

1 Look at the picture. What language are they speaking? Check your answer in the text.

_____

2 What do these numbers refer to in the text? Match 1–6 with a–f.

1 [c] a hundred
2 [ ] two billion
3 [ ] two million
4 [ ] nine hundred million
5 [ ] three hundred and eighty million
6 [ ] two thousand

a fluent speakers of Esperanto
b people who can speak some English
c magazines that people can read in Esperanto
d speakers of Esperanto as their first language
e speakers of Mandarin Chinese as a first language
f native speakers of English

3 Answer the questions. Use full sentences.

What is the origin of the name *Esperanto*?
'D-ro Esperanto' is Zamenhof's name in Esperanto.

1 What kind of language did Zamenhof want to invent?

_____

2 Which language has the most native speakers?

_____

3 In which European countries is Esperanto on school timetables?

_____

4 What are two advantages of learning Esperanto?

_____

_____

Grammar

-ing and infinitive forms

1 Complete the table with the *-ing* form of the verbs in the box.

> arrange call come dive do move put reply run say swim travel

+ *-ing*	-✗ + *-ing*
_____	*arranging*
_____	_____
_____	_____
_____	_____
double last letter + *-ing*	
_____	_____
_____	_____

-ing nouns

2 Complete the dialogue with the *-ing* noun form of the verbs in brackets.

Tina What do you think of *speaking* (speak) a second language?

Will Well, _____ (1 know) how to speak another language makes _____ (2 travel) abroad easier. _____ (3 learn) English is more useful these days than _____ (4 study) French. More people around the world speak English than French.

Tina What other advantages does _____ (5 have) a second language bring?

Will _____ (6 understand) a second language helps you to appreciate that country's culture better. _____ (7 use) the internet to get information is easier, too. _____ (8 visit) websites in other languages gives you much wider access. Oh, yes! _____ (9 go) to university and _____ (10 get) a job are also easier with a second language.

3 Complete the text with the *-ing* noun form of the verbs in the box.

> ask ~~call~~ change communicate make send use

Calling friends on a mobile phone is a daily experience for people who can hear. But **(1)** _____ a mobile is not something that you might associate with deaf people, who cannot hear. Think again!

In fact, **(2)** _____ text messages has changed the lives of millions of deaf people when they are away from home. **(3)** _____ plans to meet friends, and **(4)** _____ those plans if necessary, gives deaf people much more independence than they had ten years ago. **(5)** _____ is now something that deaf people can do independently, without **(6)** _____ for help.

Verb + *-ing* or infinitive (with *to*)

4 Match 1–6 with a–f to make sentences and questions.

1 She suggested ⬜ *b*
2 We don't want ⬜
3 Will they agree ⬜
4 They can't stand ⬜
5 Has she finished ⬜
6 I can't help you ⬜

a to pass the test.
b meeting at five.
c to play football.
d reading her book?
e to pay us £80?
f doing homework.

5 Complete the sentences with the *-ing* or infinitive form of the verbs in brackets.

Does James like *taking part in* (take part in) competitions?

1 We've decided _____ (take up) horse riding.

2 Would you miss _____ (listen to) music?

3 We have to practise _____ (read) in English.

4 Does Victoria need _____ (resit) her exams?

5 We helped the team _____ (win) the league.

6 Do you prefer _____ (speak) or _____ (write) in English?

6 Complete the dialogue with the *-ing* or infinitive form of the verbs in the box.

| choose find help read ~~translate~~ use work |

Anna What are you doing?

Brad Oh, I've agreed *to translate* this music website.

Anna Why?

Brad I enjoy (1) _____ other people with translations, but this one's really hard.

Anna Do you like (2) _____ a 'real' dictionary or do you prefer (3) _____ the hard words online?

Brad It depends. Sometimes people want the translations immediately, so I need (4) _____ quickly, and then I use an online dictionary. But actually, I love (5) _____ all of the example sentences in a real dictionary and then (6) _____ the most appropriate translations.

Consolidation

7 Complete the text with the correct form of the verbs in brackets.

Artificial communication?

With robots, *talking* (talk) like a human is now common, but is the robot 'intelligent'? For many scientists, the answer is 'yes'. According to them, _____ (**1** copy) human speech means that a robot has 'intelligence'.

However, not all scientists agree. According to these scientists, _____ (**2** have) conversations with a 'chatbot' isn't the same as _____ (**3** enjoy) an 'intelligent' conversation with a robot. A chatbot can practise _____ (**4** speak) like a human, but its conversation is normally very limited. To be intelligent, a robot must answer questions in the same way as a human.

Meet Dr Hugh Loebner, a wealthy American who loves _____ (**5** talk) to chatbots. He wanted _____ (**6** help) scientists to create an intelligent robot. So in 1990, he decided _____ (**7** start) a competition. He has agreed _____ (**8** pay) $150,000 to the creator of the world's first 'intelligent' talking robot.

Since 1990, no one has made a robot that passes the intelligence test – yet.

Communication

Vocabulary *say, talk, speak* and *tell*

1 Complete the sentences with the correct form of *say*, *talk*, *speak* or *tell*.

The teacher was *talking* about natural disasters.

1 _____ English is easy.
2 I couldn't hear you. What did you _____?
3 Please don't _____ my parents.
4 He always _____ lies.
5 What are you _____ about?
6 Do you _____ French?

Learning a language

2 Find the words and complete the sentences.

You can learn through *repetition* (epretoniti).

1 Have you got a good _____ (remmoy)?
2 I always _____ (serive) before a test.
3 Do we have to _____ (lartantes) this?
4 We need to _____ (serimome) these irregular verbs.
5 I hate grammar _____ (raceptic)!
6 My big sister is a university _____ (detstun).

Telephoning

3 Complete the dialogue with the correct nouns or form of the verbs.

Tom   I decided to p*hone* Georgia but her number was (1) e_____.
I called again, but I (2) g_____ a w_____ n_____.
Harriet How do you know?
Tom   A man (3) a_____ the p_____. So then I tried to (4) g_____ t_____ for a third time. But she'd gone out and she'd (5) p_____ on the a_____ p_____. In the end, I just (6) l_____ a m_____.

Extension MOBILE PHONES

4 Find nine nouns in the wordsquare and complete the dialogues.

BAT	CHAR	AS	YOU	LO
SI	S̶E̶T̶	CO	GO	GER
RACT	GN	PHO	TONE	D̶S̶
PAY	RING	AL	CRE	TE
DO	H̶A̶N̶	NE	F̶R̶E̶E̶	DIT
H̶E̶A̶D̶	WN	NT	AD	RY

A Why are you talking to your MP3 player?
B I'm not! I've got a hands-free headset.
C My (1) b _ _ _ _ _ 's low.
D Do you want my (2) p _ _ _ _ c _ _ _ _ _ _ ?
E Wow! Where did you get the special (3) r _ _ _ _ _ _ _ ?
F It's a (4) d _ _ _ _ _ _ _ from the internet.
G Oh, no. I haven't got any (5) c _ _ _ _ _ .
H Use my phone. I'm on a (6) c _ _ _ _ _ _ _ , not (7) p _ _ - a _ - y _ _ - g _ .
I Oh, no. I haven't got a s (8) _ _ _ _ _ .
J Look, I've got three bars. Take my phone.

Speaking Making a phone call

5 Choose the correct answer.

Mandy Hi, Mandy **saying** / (**speaking.**)
Phil   Hi, it's me, Phil.
Mandy Phil! Where have you been? Your mobile's been (1) **engaged** / **wrong** for hours.
Phil   Did you (2) **leave** / **make** a message?
Mandy No, because when I finally (3) **put on** / **got through**, I didn't have any more (4) **credit** / **contract!** I only had 30 seconds of talk-time, so I didn't have time to (5) **say** / **tell** anything.
Phil   So what did you want to (6) **say** / **talk**?
Mandy It's too late now. I wanted (7) **asking** / **to ask** you about our project.
Phil   OK. what's the problem?
Mandy Never mind. I asked Mark instead.

Writing

An opinion essay

1 Read the paragraph. What is the writer's opinion?

_____

Some people disagree, but I strongly believe that (trebetinhgsaoltively) the government should ban eating chewing gum in public places. _____ (**1** pinoniminyo), chewing gum makes a horrible mess when people drop it. It is very difficult to remove chewing gum from the streets and in most cities, the streets have small black and white spots from used chewing gum. _____ (**2** sakefiyomu), chewing gum can also ruin our shoes and clothes.

_____ (**3** rasfoceasdinmencar), people should chew gum at home or in their car, but not in the street. _____ (**4** hinhakinyteftiditelt) our cities would be cleaner if chewing gum was prohibited in public places.

Introducing opinions

2 Complete the paragraph with the expressions for introducing opinions.

3 Do you agree with the writer's opinion?

I really agree that ... OR
I don't really agree that ...

_____
_____
_____

4 Match the opinions in the box with 1–3.

it is bad quality   they are dangerous
it gives you diseases   it is expensive
they are expensive   they are noisy
it makes you fat   it smells   it is unhealthy

1 fast food   it is bad quality,

_____, _____

2 motorbikes _____,

_____, _____

3 smoking _____,

_____, _____

5 Write a paragraph about fast food, motorbikes or smoking. Use the expressions from exercise 2 and the ideas from exercise 4.

_____
_____
_____
_____
_____
_____
_____
_____
_____
_____
_____
_____
_____
_____
_____

Quick check

Vocabulary

1 **Choose the correct answer.**

1 Have I **said** / **told** you my joke?
2 I didn't **say** / **speak** anything.
3 Can I **say** / **speak** to you?
4 Be quiet. I'm **talking** / **saying**.

2 **Complete the sentences with words for learning a language.**

1 Have you done enough rev_____ yet?
2 You aren't stud_____ very hard this term!
3 Listen to the CD and rep_____ the words.
4 Can you trans_____ this?
5 You need to do more prac_____.

3 **Complete the sentences with the telephoning words in the box.**

answered engaged got through left put on

1 I _____ the answer phone and went out.
2 They were _____ when we called.
3 She called but nobody _____.
4 I _____ a message on the answer phone.
5 Finally, he _____ to her.

Vocabulary review: Units 1–4

4 **Complete the sentences with the words in the box.**

energetic exhausting getting legs revise revising stomach-ache tap water win

1 I don't like (a) _____ for exams, but I love (b) _____ high marks! That's why I always (c) _____.
2 You need to be very (a) _____ and have strong (b) _____ to (c) _____ a marathon. Marathons are (d) _____.
3 You can get a (a) _____ from drinking the (b) _____ in some countries. Be careful!

Grammar

5 **Complete the sentences with the -ing noun form of the verbs in the box.**

get pass ski swim visit win

1 In winter, France is popular for _____.
2 All athletes dream of _____ important races.
3 _____ a wrong number is annoying.
4 I always dream of _____ Hollywood.
5 _____ this year's exams was harder than I'd expected.
6 _____ is good for your health.

6 **Complete the sentences with the -ing or infinitive form of the verbs.**

1 I hate _____ (wait) for buses.
2 We agreed _____ (meet) on Tuesday.
3 Let's practise _____ (sing) it again.
4 Do you miss _____ (live) by the sea?
5 Paul wants _____ (get through) to his mum.

Grammar review: Units 1–4

7 **Choose the correct answers**

They (1) **hadn't** / **haven't** invented the internet when most adults were children. But now, the internet (2) **has become** / **became** the major means of communication for the young. (3) **Owning** / **Own** a mobile is common: in the UK, 96% of teenagers have one, according to a poll. But, although only 60% of teenagers (4) **are allowed to** / **must** use the internet at home, they enjoy (5) **spending** / **to spend** longer online than on their mobile. Every week, an average sixteen-year-old (6) **has to** / **might** spend seven hours online. (7) **Doing** / **To do** research for homework often takes half of this time and the rest is chatting to friends.

However, few young people want (8) **reading** / **to read** the news online. More than 50% like (9) **reading** / **to read** a newspaper. Most prefer (10) **use** / **using** the internet for communication.

5 | One world

Reading

1 Read the text quickly and label the photos.

1 solar panels

2 _____

3 _____

A burning problem

A The Earth's population is expanding. There are 6.5 billion people on Earth today. By 2030, there will be 8 billion people.

B Every day, we produce a lot of carbon dioxide. More people means that the Earth's carbon dioxide emissions will also increase. And the problems of global warming will get worse, too.

C We enjoy driving our cars. We like a cool drink in summer and a warm house in winter. We like flying to go on holiday. And we love buying products. Most of the things that we enjoy use electricity or petrol. When we use our car, it burns petrol. Burning petrol creates carbon dioxide. To produce electricity, we burn coal, gas or oil. Burning coal, gas and oil also creates carbon dioxide.

D We understand the problems that carbon dioxide causes, but we find it hard to change our lifestyle. However, we should remember that the lifestyle of some animals has already changed. For example, thousands of polar bears have died because the polar ice is forming later in the year. The bears need the ice to hunt, so they are starving because they cannot find food. How many more will die before we stop global warming?

E Doing nothing is not an option. So, what should we do? Making electricity without creating carbon dioxide is one idea. Solar panels and wind turbines provide carbon-free electricity. We can use bio-fuel (vegetable oil) instead of petrol or diesel in car and truck engines, too. Burning vegetable oil does not create carbon dioxide. But, although the alternatives to oil and gas will help, they are not going to produce enough power for our future.

F Using less electricity and using less petrol are the only real solutions. That means people cycling more and flying less. It also means reusing more and buying fewer products. This is easy to say, but who wants to be the first? Nobody does. That is why agreements such as the Kyoto Protocol are important. The only solution to this problem is for everyone to work together, internationally.

2 Read the text again. Are these things part of the problem (*P*) or part of the solution (*S*)?

cars	P	4 reusing	
1 cool drinks		5 solar energy	
2 cycling		6 warm houses	
3 planes		7 wind power	

3 Answer the questions. Use full sentences.

How is the number of people on Earth changing?
The population is expanding.

1 Why will the Earth's carbon dioxide emissions rise?

_____

_____

2 How do cars produce carbon dioxide?

_____

_____

3 Give an example of the effects of global warming on animals.

_____

_____

4 How can we make electricity without creating carbon dioxide?

_____

_____

5 What is the only way we can solve the problem of global warming?

Grammar

Future forms *will*

1 **Put the words in the correct order to make sentences and questions.**

take up / tennis / will / you / next year?
Will you take up tennis next year?

1 you / we / help / in a moment / 'll

_____

2 they / the match / win / will / tomorrow

_____

3 time / you / what / will / arrive?

_____

4 people / lifestyles? / will / change / their

_____

5 won't / this DVD / like / you

_____

6 soon? / see / will / her / you

_____

2 **Complete the sentences with the *will* form of the verbs in the box.**

| not arrive | be | cycle | feel | finish | leave |
| not make | not pass | ~~not tell~~ | not use | win |

Your secret is safe. We *won't tell* anyone.

1 I _____ here at seven, I promise. I _____ late.

2 _____ she _____ a message for us?

3 Stop, or you _____ sick.

4 If you don't revise more for your exams, you _____.

5 They're a great team. I think that they _____.

6 _____ you _____ your homework tomorrow?

7 It's very near. I _____. I _____ the car.

8 I _____ my bed now because I want to go to sleep again.

going to

3 **Write sentences with the *going to* future.**

they / not take part in / the race
They aren't going to take part in the race.

1 you / go / to the cinema later?

_____

2 my mum / phone / my aunt tonight

_____

3 they / train / this evening?

_____

4 my brother / not resit / his exams

_____

5 the fans / ask for / a new coach?

_____

4 **Complete the sentences with the *going to* or *will* form of the verbs in brackets.**

Look at that rain! It's *going to flood* (flood) soon.

1 Oh, no! We've finished all the coffee. OK, I _____ (get) some more.

2 He's gone to the bookshop. He _____ _____ (buy) a dictionary.

3 Look! He _____ (give) her those flowers.

4 I think that I _____ (live) in New York one day.

5 I _____ (phone) this weekend, OK?

6 _____ (you / play) volleyball with them again on Saturday?

Present continuous

5 Look at the diary and complete the dialogue with the *will* or present continuous form of the verbs in brackets.

15 Monday	badminton practice
16 Tuesday	cinema - 7 p.m.
17 Wednesday	English test revision
18 Thursday	English test - 10 a.m.
19 Friday	
20 Saturday	football practice
21 Sunday	lunch at Grandma's

Ian Let's go for a ride this week. *Are you doing* (you / do) anything on Saturday?

Leo Yes, I _____ (**1 play**) football.

Ian Right. _____ (**2 plan**) anything for Sunday?

Leo Yes, we _____ (**3 have**) lunch at my grandma's.

Ian OK. What time do you think that you _____ (**4 get**) home?

Leo It's usually quite late.

Ian Oh, I see. What about after school? What _____ (**5 you / do**) on Tuesday?

Leo Well, I _____ (**6 go**) to the cinema at seven.

Ian When _____ (**7 the film / finish**), do you know? Can we go out after that?

Leo I don't think so. It _____ probably _____ (**8 finish**) at about nine, so we _____ (**9 not have**) time on Tuesday. But I _____ (**10 not do**) anything on Thursday or Friday after school. Are you free then?

Ian Yes. Let's go on Thursday.

Consolidation

6 Complete the dialogue with the words in the box.

> am I going to change   am I going to put
> aren't going to have   are you going to reduce
> ~~are you flying~~   'll be   'll buy   'll look
> 're catching   will create   will organise
> will reduce   won't need

Yasmina When are you flying?

Jacqui At six o'clock so we (**1**) _____ the airport bus at three.

Yasmina Oh, I'll help you. It (**2**) _____ easier with three people.

Jacqui It's OK, thanks. We (**3**) _____ _____ a lot of luggage so we (**4**) _____ help.

Yasmina OK. By the way, how (**5**) _____ _____ the pollution from your flights?

Jacqui What do you mean? Don't be silly!

Yasmina It isn't silly. Planes create much more pollution than trains and buses.

Jacqui Yes, but how (**6**) _____ _____ that?

Yasmina You can plant trees. Trees reduce greenhouse gases so buying trees (**7**) _____ the effect of the pollution from your flight.

Jacqui OK, OK, I (**8**) _____ a tree! But where (**9**) _____ _____ it? I live in a flat, remember?

Yasmina You don't have to plant the trees at home. You buy them online from a carbon-reduction company and they (**10**) _____ it for you.

Jacqui Why do I have to buy more than one?

Yasmina Look at the website! Your flight (**11**) _____ a lot of pollution. Most flights create about a kilo of carbon per passenger per kilometre!

Jacqui OK. I (**12**) _____ at the website at home, but I need to finish packing now.

Communication

Vocabulary Environmental change

1 Complete the sentences with the words in the box.

> burning creates droughts effects emissions
> ~~floods~~ freezes global warming is melting
> are rising is rising

Rising sea levels will cause *floods*.

1 _____ oil and gas _____ pollution.
2 The Earth's temperature _____.
   We call this _____.
3 The _____ of low rainfall
   include _____ in southern Europe.
4 _____ from cars increase
   global warming.
5 Sea levels _____ because ice
   at the North and South Poles _____.
6 Water _____ and becomes ice at 0°C.

Weather collocations

2 Complete the key with the words in the box.
Then match the key with the weather symbols
on the map.

> light ~~a little~~ severe strong

Key

a *little* snow | [a] | 2 _____ sun | [ ]
1 _____ showers [ ] | 3 _____ storms [ ]

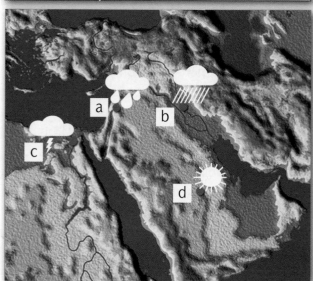

Extension WEATHER: ADJECTIVES

3 Find the opposites of the adjectives in the
wordsquare.

sunny   c l o u d y   3 rainy   d _ y
1 foggy   c _ _ _ r   4 warm   c _ _ _ _ y
2 freezing   b _ _ _ _ _ g 5 windy   c _ _ m

D	R	I	C	L	O	U	D	Y	C	S
B	I	C	S	O	S	T	C	A	L	M
C	B	O	I	L	I	N	G	A	E	R
J	O	T	E	X	A	S	T	S	A	Y
O	C	H	I	L	L	Y	S	D	R	Y

4 Complete the sentences with the adjectives from
exercise 3.

It's *chilly* at night, but warmer in the daytime.
1 Cycling is good in calm weather, but it's harder in
   _____ weather.
2 It's _____ in Bangkok in April. It's 38°C
   every day!
3 It's often _____ in the valley in the
   mornings, but the sun means that it's
   _____ on the tops of the hills.
4 The UK isn't very sunny in winter. It's
   _____ nearly every day.
5 You won't need an umbrella. It's going to be
   _____ today.

Speaking Discussing the weather

5 Number the dialogue in the correct order.

a [ ] Really? Is it going to change then?
      It was freezing last night!

b [ ] Chilly? No, this forecast says that it'll be
      quite warm.

c [ ] Is cloudy weather warmer than clear
      weather at night?

d [1] It's going to be chilly tomorrow, isn't it?

e [ ] Yes. The clouds trap the heat and make it
      warmer.

f [ ] It was only freezing because it was clear
      during the day.

Writing

A postcard Order of adjectives

1 Read the postcard and complete the table with the **bold** adjectives and nouns.

Dear Luke

My uncle's farm is fascinating. Everything here is so BIG! He's got a **huge, old, black, American Cadillac** – but guess what? He's going to sell it because it's bad for the environment! He's got an **old, Indian, leather, fishing canoe** and loads of other amazing things as well.

My uncle and aunt live in a **beautiful, big, white, wooden house** with a balcony all around it. You must come with me and visit them one day!

See you,

Daniel

Luke Taylor

78 Links Road

Milehome

Pipperfield

NG10 4HB

UK

Order of adjectives

	opinion ➜	size ➜	age ➜	colour ➜	origin ➜	material ➜	purpose ➜	noun
1	—	huge						
2								
3								

2 Rewrite the text of the postcard with the adjectives in the correct order.

This morning we went mountain biking on (bikes / black / mountain / carbon-fibre / Trek). Tomorrow we're going on the road with (**1** Orbea / racing / bikes / new / aluminium).

The day after tomorrow we're learning to scuba-dive! We have to sit at the bottom of a (**2** blue / swimming / deep / pool) and practise breathing. We have to wear a (**3** tank / yellow / air / big / metal) and (**4** rubber / wetsuits / black).

Our hotel's next to a (**5** beach / white / sandy / really beautiful / long). Are there still (**6** clouds / black / heavy) at home?

This morning we went mountain biking on black, Trek, carbon-fibre, mountain bikes. Tomorrow _____

_____

_____

_____

_____

_____

_____

_____

_____

_____

_____

_____

_____

Quick check

Vocabulary

1 Complete the sentences with the correct form of the verbs for environmental change.

1 Global warming means that the Earth's temperature is r_____.
2 We c_____ carbon dioxide by burning coal, gas and oil.
3 Plants g_____ best in warm, sunny climates.
4 The polar ice will m_____ more and more quickly.
5 Sea levels are going up and a lot of rivers will f_____.
6 Global warming a_____ everyone.

2 Choose the correct answer.

1 There's been **cool / thick** snow in Andorra.
2 Light **fog / rain** can freeze on roads to form ice.
3 There's a **high / gentle** breeze today.
4 The wind and rain quickly became a **severe / thick** storm.
5 You can't see very far in thick **fog / wind**.
6 I don't mind **high / light** showers.

Vocabulary review: Units 1–5

3 Complete the text with the words in the box.

> active   computer game   MP3 player   making
> marks   race   taking part in   train

Most people enjoy relaxation: lying down and listening to their (1) _____, watching TV, or perhaps (2) _____ a few phone calls. But (3) _____ people don't like sitting down for long. They (4) _____ at the gym or practise their favourite sports. They like (5) _____ competitions and they usually prefer winning a (6) _____ to getting to the next level on a (7) _____. They don't like losing in anything that they do, so at school they often get good (8) _____, too.

Grammar

4 Complete the sentences with the *going to* or *will* form of the verbs in brackets.

1 Look at that bag! _____ (it/fall)?
2 We _____ (not meet) Mark after school today; he's busy.
3 I _____ (help) you later, I promise.
4 _____ (you/win) the race today?
5 Do you think that _____ (we/arrive) before it finishes?
6 Science is easy. We _____ (not revise) for the test.

5 Complete the dialogue with the present continuous or *will* form of the verbs in brackets.

Tina   _____ (1 you / meet) John at seven o'clock?

Frank No, but I think we _____ (2 talk) to him tomorrow instead. He _____ (3 finish) school at three and he _____ (4 not go) to his grandparents' house until five. So I think that tomorrow afternoon _____ (5 not be) a problem. We _____ (6 have) time after school.

Grammar review: Units 1–5

6 Complete the text with the words in the box.

> can't be   had caused   have told
> haven't listened   must stop   to do   to sell

Scientists (1) _____ us about global warming for years, but we (2) _____. We (3) _____ producing so much carbon dioxide. On the radio, they said that global warming (4) _____ floods. I thought, 'It (5) _____ true.' But it was true. I wanted (6) _____ something, so I decided (7) _____ my car and I bought a bike. I love it! And for longer journeys, I take the train.

Reading

A mysterious quake

A At 7,687,000 km², Australia is more than seven times bigger than Egypt. It is **huge**. If you drive the 4,100 km from Sydney to Perth, it will take you 50 hours! Even a flight takes five hours. About 85% of Australia's 20 million inhabitants live on the coast, where the climate is good. The central 'outback' areas of Australia are mainly desert. On long-distance journeys by road, you might not see another person for hours, or even days.

Australia is also a place where strange things happen ...

B A seismograph is a machine that measures earthquakes. At 11.03 p.m. on 28 May 1993, seismographs in Australia registered a very large and unusual shock in the outback of Western Australia. For scientists, this was fascinating. The vibrations were as big as some earthquakes, but they were different.

If a vibration like this happened in Europe, buildings would collapse and thousands of people would die. But in the outback, the explosion had not affected anyone. In fact, because the outback is so huge, only a few people actually noticed it. 'The ground moved,' said one miner. 'It was late at night, but for a second the sky was bright, like daytime,' another man remembered.

C The only explanation was that a meteorite had crashed into the desert. Meteorites make craters which are easy to see, but the scientists investigated an area the size of England and could not find anything. Everyone soon forgot about it.

D Then, in March 1995, police in Japan arrested members of the Aum Shinrikyo terrorist group. The police discovered that, in 1993, the group had bought a large farm called Banjawarn Station, 600 km east of Perth.

E Australian police confirmed that the group had visited Western Australia in May 1993. They continued their investigation, and what they discovered at Banjawarn Station was astonishing. Aum Shinrikyo had mined uranium and made a nuclear bomb. Then they had exploded it!

F Can a country be so big and empty that it is possible to explode a nuclear bomb? And no one realises for more than two years? The answer is 'Yes'. Strange – but true!

---

1 **Read the text. Are the sentences true or false? Explain your answers.**

It takes fifty hours to fly from Sydney to Perth.
False. It takes fifty hours to drive or six hours to fly.

1 The majority of Australians do not live in the outback.
_____

2 Central Australia is mainly chilly and foggy.
_____

3 Scientists discovered a crater the size of England.
_____

4 Aum Shinrikyo bought Banjawarn Station in 1995.
_____

5 Aum Shinrikyo built a nuclear bomb.
_____

2 **Answer the questions. Use full sentences.**

What is the population of Australia?
The population of Australia is 20 million.

1 What effects of the shock did local people feel or see?
_____

2 How can scientists find where a meteorite has crashed?
_____

3 Is Banjawarn Station closer to Sydney or Perth?
_____

4 How long did the bomb remain a secret?
_____

Grammar

Conditionals

1 Match the rules a–c with the sentences 1–6.

a	Zero conditional We use the zero conditional to talk about general truths.
b	First conditional We use the first conditional to talk about a possible future event which is probable.
c	Second conditional We use the second conditional to talk about a situation which is imaginary.

1 If you leave a message, she'll call you back. `b`
2 Droughts will get worse if we don't reduce global warming. ☐
3 I'd tell you if I knew the answer. ☐
4 You wear a jacket if it's chilly. ☐
5 If I'm thirsty, I drink milk. ☐
6 I would choose Chinese if I could learn another language. ☐

Zero conditional

2 Complete the text with the zero conditional form of the verbs in brackets.

If I _am_ (be) asleep, my sister always _goes_ (go) to bed quietly. But if I _____ (1 not be) asleep, she _____ (2 talk) to me. If we _____ (3 chat) for a long time, we _____ (4 not feel) tired. And if we _____ (5 not feel) tired, we _____ (6 not go) to sleep easily. I _____ (7 not like) reading if it _____ (8 be) late. But if my sister _____ (9 not feel) tired, she usually _____ (10 read) a book for a few hours. That's why she reads so many books. And that's why I'm always tired in the mornings!

3 Write the zero conditional sentences.

if / you / pay £3 / the machine / give / you / two tickets / ?
If you pay £3, does the machine give you two tickets?

1 she / usually / have / some tea / if / she / be / thirsty

_____

_____

2 if / you / phone / after eleven / he / not answer

_____

_____

3 we / not go out / if / we / not have / much money

_____

_____

4 it / flood / in Bangkok / if / it / rain / a lot / ?

_____

_____

5 he / take / an aspirin / if / he / have / a headache

_____

_____

First or second conditional?

4 Complete the sentences with the first conditional form of the verbs in brackets.

Rory   Don't worry. If you _revise_ (revise) all day, you_'ll_ _pass_ (pass) your exams.

Milly   Really? I _____ (1 not be) happy if I _____ (2 not pass) them. What _____ (3 happen) if I _____ (4 fail)?

Rory   Well, if you _____ (5 fail) the exams, you _____ (6 resit) them next year.

Milly   I know, but if I _____ (7 not pass), we _____ (8 be) in different years at school.

Rory   I know! If I _____ (9 not go) now, you _____ (10 not revise). So I'm going. Bye!

5 Correct the mistake in each second conditional sentence.

They won't win if they didn't train every evening.
They wouldn't win if they didn't train every evening.

1 She would get better marks if she listens in class.

_____

2 I not use a bike very much if I didn't cycle to school.

_____
_____

3 I sent a text if I had some credit.

_____

4 You play for England if you were Beckham?

_____

5 He would lend you his book if he would have it at school.

_____
_____

6 Would you helped me with my homework if I asked you?

_____
_____

6 Complete the sentences with the first or second conditional form of the verbs in the box.

not call   memorise   practise   put on   ~~read~~
not say   not win

Will you *read* the book if you enjoy the film?

1 We _____ if we don't train a lot.
2 He'd be sad if you _____ 'Hello'.
3 What would you think if she _____ you?
4 If the list wasn't so long, they _____ it.
5 _____ she _____ the guitar if she had more free time?
6 If I am busy this afternoon, I _____ the answer phone.

7 Decide if the action in each sentence is probable or imaginary. Then write sentences in the first or second conditional.

she / go / swimming / if / it / be / sunny today
She'll go swimming if it's sunny today.

1 you / be / surprised / snow / in Cairo?

_____

2 if / Michael Owen / not score / again / Newcastle / not win / the match

_____
_____

3 I / be / amazed / if / our team / win / the match

_____
_____

4 they / not watch / *The Simpsons* / if / they / get / home late

_____
_____

Consolidation

8 Choose the correct answers.

Nirg   If you go into the red building, you **'d see /
(**'ll see**) three doors. You can ask for help
here, but you'll get a higher score if you
(1) don't / won't ask. If you **(2) open /
opened** the first door, you go down a long
tunnel. I **(3) won't / wouldn't** go that way
if I were you.

Sty   What would happen if I **(4) chose / choose**
the second door?

Nirg   If you go through the second door, you'll
(5) saw / see a light in the distance. If you
(6) collected / collect the light, you get
250 points. But it's really difficult, so the
third door is the best.

Sty   OK. … Oh, no! I didn't see the human!

Communication

Vocabulary False friends

1 Complete the crossword.

Down ↓	Across →
1 help	4 achieve something
2 really	6 put onto a CD, DVD, etc
3 important	7 big
5 mislead	9 rational
8 understand	

```
¹A        ²          ³
⁴S                   
 S              ⁵     
 I         ⁶         
 S                   
 T     ⁷   ⁸         




     ⁹              
```

get and make

2 Complete the sentences with the words in the box.

> a cold   into trouble   in touch with   money
> ready   sure   ~~up your mind~~

If you make *up your mind* which CD you want, I'll buy it for you now.

1 She often gets _____ with teachers at school.

2 It's freezing! If you don't put on a jumper, you'll get _____ .

3 I want to make lots of _____ one day!

4 She's getting _____ . Can you wait for a few minutes?

5 Always make _____ that you've answered all the questions.

6 He gets _____ his cousins by email.

Extension DO AND HAVE

3 Match 1–7 with a–g to make sentences.

1 The internet can have [f]
2 Can I have ☐
3 I'm doing ☐
4 My doctor has ☐
5 The research has had ☐
6 They haven't done ☐
7 Will you do ☐

a an art course this term.
b lots of sympathy for me.
c an effect on the government.
d a look at your magazine?
e me a favour?
f a negative influence.
g any research on the new virus.

Speaking Giving advice (2)

4 Match the problems 1–5 with the suggestions a–e. Then choose the correct answer.

1 [b] 'I need to **do** / make a call. Can I use your phone?'

2 ☐ 'I'm always late and I **get** / **make** into trouble.'

3 ☐ 'I hate **revising** / **resitting** vocabulary lists.'

4 ☐ 'I'm annoyed because I never **win** / **lose**.'

5 ☐ 'If I **'ll play** / **play** a computer game after dinner, I forget the time and I go to bed very late.'

a 'Why don't you train every day if you **want** / **wanted** to win?'

b 'I haven't got one, sorry. I **'d** / **'ll** use the phone in the café if I were you.'

c 'If I **am** / **were** you, I'd memorise just ten words every week. Repeat the ten words twice a day.'

d 'If you set the alarm on your computer's calendar, you'll **record** / **remember** to go to bed.'

e 'Why not set two alarm clocks? If you **'ll put** / **put** one under the bed, you'll have to get up and turn it off!'

A picture story

1 Match the words 1–4 with the labels in the picture a–d.

1 [a] bumper   3 [ ] chain
2 [ ] cashpoint machine   4 [ ] number plate

2 Read the sentences opposite and match the words 1–10 with the spaces a–j. Then write the sentences with the correct picture in the story.

1 'd have   6 Have you lost
2 drove   7 tried
3 had pulled   8 robbed
4 hadn't opened   9 was looking out
5 happened   10 were relaxing

They (**a**) [ ] to pull the front off the cashpoint machine. Nothing (**b**) [ ], so they tried again. Suddenly, the car jumped forwards.

Sim connected the bumper and the cashpoint machine with a chain while Dom (**c**) [ ] for the police.

Sim and Dom (**d**) [ ] away very quickly.

Two hours later, while they (**e**) [ ] at home, the doorbell rang. '(**f**) [ ] a number plate, sir?' asked a policeman.

Sim and Dom parked next to the cashpoint machine. 'If we (**g**) [ ] that, we (**h**) [ ] a lot of money!' said Sim.

They looked at the cashpoint machine – but it was still there! Sim investigated. The chain (**i**) [ ] the bumper off the car, but it (**j**) [ ] the cashpoint machine!

_____
_____
_____

_____
_____
_____

_____
_____
_____

_____
_____
_____

_____
_____
_____

_____
_____
_____

Quick check

Vocabulary

1 **Choose the correct answer.**

1 I love your **large / long** hair.
2 Did he **carry out / realise** the research?
3 I can never **record / remember** her name.
4 Revision is a **sensible / sensitive** idea.

2 **Complete the sentences with *get* or *make*.**

1 Some singers only want to _____ money.
2 They usually _____ tired before half past ten.
3 If you _____ a plan, it will all be fine.
4 Hurry up! _____ up your mind!
5 He must _____ an effort this term.
6 We _____ into trouble all the time.
7 _____ ready! We're waiting!
8 I'll _____ in touch with her soon.

Vocabulary review: Units 1–6

3 **Answer the questions with the words in the box.**

clock decide drought easy-going fantastic
help jug miss -opener practise suggest
tiny want water

1 Find the opposites of these words.
   a huge _____   c flood _____
   b awful _____   d anxious _____
2 Complete the compound nouns.
   a alarm _____   c tin _____
   b tap _____   d water _____
3 After which verbs do we use the *-ing* form?
   a _____   c _____
   b _____
4 After which verbs do we use the infinitive form?
   a _____   c _____
   b _____

Grammar

4 **Complete the sentences with the zero conditional form of the verbs in the box.**

drop fall fail get say not set wake up
not win

1 She _____ angry if she _____.
2 If you _____ a ball, it _____.
3 What _____ your parents _____ if you _____ any of your exams?
4 I _____ late if I _____ my alarm clock.

5 **Complete the sentences with the first or second conditional form of the verbs in brackets.**

1 If we had enough money, we _____ (take up) skiing.
2 Will you _____ (lend) me your book if I need it?
3 They wouldn't get into trouble if they _____ (not play) loud music.
4 I _____ (revise) for the English test if I were you.
5 If we don't train, we _____ (not win) the next race.
6 Would we create less pollution if we _____ (drive) less?

Grammar review: Units 1–6

6 **Choose the correct answers.**

Alex (1) **had been / went** at work all week and he (2) **has needed / needed** to get some food. When he had finished (3) **to shop / shopping**, he walked back to his car.

Suddenly, he noticed that someone (4) **had driven / drove** into it and then he saw a note that someone (5) **was leaving / had left** on the car window.

'It (6) **can't / must** be the person who drove into the car,' he thought. He read the note:

'If I leave this, people (7) **will / would** think that it's my name and address. But if I (8) **do / did** that, I would have to pay. So I won't. Sorry. Goodbye!'

Revision: Units 4-6

Vocabulary

1 Choose the correct answer.

1 I wasn't **talking** / **telling**.
2 Who **said** / **told** 'Hello'?
3 **Say** / **Tell** me your name.
4 We don't **speak** / **talk** Japanese.
5 Please **say** / **speak** something.
6 I'll **say** / **talk** to your teacher later.

2 Complete the sentences with words for learning a language and telephoning.

1 R_____ means saying something again and again.
2 Exam r_____ is really boring.
3 Do you p_____ writing once a week?
4 I had to t_____ a dialogue into English.
5 My sister is a university s_____.
6 I tried to g_____ t_____ t_____ you, but your number was e_____.

3 Complete the text with the environment and weather words in the box.

disappear droughts floods global grow
heavy melt rise severe strong

The effects of (1) _____ warming have begun. (2) _____ storms with (3) _____ rain and very (4) _____ winds are more common now. The ice at the poles will (5) _____ in the next 100 years and sea levels will (6) _____. This will cause (7) _____ in low-lying countries such as Bangladesh. Some Pacific islands will completely (8) _____. In other places, the weather will be drier. There will be (9) _____ and it will be difficult for farmers to (10) _____ food.

4 Choose the correct words from the box to complete the sentences. (Do not use the false friends.)

actually adults attend assist compromises
commitments deceive disappoint majors
now

1 I have two _____ today.
2 They didn't _____ the meeting.
3 Do you live there _____?
4 This is for children, not for _____.
5 Did the ending of that novel _____ you?

5 Complete the sentences with the correct form of *get* or *make*.

1 She never _____ bored in the school holidays.
2 I'll call her and I'll _____ sure.
3 I'm going to _____ ready now.
4 It was good, but I _____ tired by 10 p.m.
5 We _____ really excited when we have a match.
6 It's difficult, but you have to _____ an effort.

6 Choose the correct answers.

Revision tips

Is your (1) **memory** / **memorise** perfect? Can you (2) **record** / **remember** every word you read? Of course not! (3) **Actually** / **Now**, no one can. Don't worry: read our advice and (4) **get** / **make** ready for your exams!

- Interruptions can (5) **affect** / **effect** your revision, so (6) **create** / **expand** a quiet environment. Don't always (7) **answer** / **engage** the phone. (8) **Make up** / **Put on** the answer phone.
- Don't simply (9) **repeat** / **repetition** long lists. Look at English websites or (10) **talk** / **tell** to a friend in English.

Grammar

1 Complete the text with the *-ing* noun form of the verbs in the box.

> change cycle drive find heat live ride warm

Carbon-neutral

(1) _____ solutions to reduce global (2) _____ is the most urgent international problem. (3) _____ modern lifestyles means that we're creating more and more carbon dioxide (CO_2).

Some things in our lifestyle are important: (4) _____ our houses in winter, for example. This creates CO_2, but we would be freezing without it.

Other things, we can change. In the UK, about 25% of our CO_2 comes from (5) _____ cars. (6) _____ how and where we live or work means that, in the future, we won't need to move around our cities as much. And if we need to get from A to B, let's not forget the cleverest solution of them all. (7) _____ is cheap, it's healthy – and bikes are 'carbon-neutral'. (8) _____ a bicycle doesn't produce any CO_2.

2 Complete the sentences with the *-ing* or infinitive form of the verbs in brackets.

1 I can't stand _____ (sit) in the car for a long time.
2 Wait, she hasn't finished _____ (speak).
3 I enjoy _____ (help) my friends.
4 She loves _____ (read) magazines.
5 Does he prefer _____ (play) or _____ (watch) football?
6 I want _____ (practise) speaking English.
7 They suggested _____ (talk) to the police.
8 We decided _____ (catch) the bus to school.

3 Match the sentences 1–6 with the future uses a–f.

1 We're going to revise a lot for the exams. ☐
2 I'll never lie to you. ☐
3 Wait. I'll come too. ☐
4 It's cloudy. It isn't going to be hot today. ☐
5 They'll get married soon. ☐
6 We're meeting at five o'clock. ☐

a making a prediction based on present evidence
b talking about a definite future arrangement
c making a decision at the time of speaking
d talking about a plan or future intention
e making a prediction about the future
f making a promise

4 Complete the sentences with the *going to* or *will* form of the verbs in brackets.

1 There's only 100 metres until the finish line. Number 21 _____ (win)!
2 Oh, it's raining. I _____ (not wear) my sandals today.
3 We _____ (see) my aunt in Italy.
4 It's freezing. It _____ (snow) tonight.
5 We _____ (ski) every day of the holiday.
6 I _____ (not forget), I promise.
7 _____ (you / take up) basketball next term?
8 We _____ (use) more robots at home in the future.

5 Complete the dialogue with the present continuous or *will* form of the verbs in brackets.

Amy What time _____ (**1** you / be) here tomorrow?

Duncan Let me check my calendar …
I _____ (**2** not leave) work until seven tomorrow. Then I _____ (**3** meet) Dr Lee at half past seven.

Amy What time _____ (**4** your meeting / finish)?

Duncan We _____ (**5** not know) until tomorrow evening, sorry.

Amy OK. _____ (**6** you / send) a text, then?

Duncan Well, I _____ (**7** phone) you. It's easier than sending a text.

Amy Fine. We _____ (**8** wait) for your call.

6 Complete the sentences with the zero conditional form of the verbs in the box.

| be buy call not do eat feel not flood |
| get pass rise talk trap |

1 If you _____ too much chocolate, you _____ sick.

2 The river _____ if the rain _____ quite light.

3 _____ your parents _____ a present for you if you _____ all of your exams?

4 If she _____ me at the weekend, we _____ for a long time.

5 Greenhouse gases _____ warm air if it _____.

6 _____ you _____ into trouble if you _____ your homework?

7 Complete the sentences with the first or second conditional form of the verbs in brackets.

1 If you watch TV all night, you _____ (not pass) the test.

2 If you _____ (fail) your exams, you'd have to resit them.

3 How _____ (you / feel) if your parents knew?

4 I _____ (not say) anything if I didn't know the answer.

5 Take a coat! You _____ (get) a sore throat if you go out in the fog.

8 Choose the correct answers.

Frankie Welcome to Money-makers, the show for people who want (**1**) **making / to make** £1 million! And here's John. Now, if the questions (**2**) **are / will be** difficult, will you answer them correctly?

John Oh, yes, Frankie! I can't stand (**3**) **to lose / losing**, so I (**4**) **'m going to win / 'm winning** this show.

Frankie OK, question number one: 'If you (**5**) **speak / spoke** Dutch, where would you probably come from?' Is it …
A: Denmark, B: Germany, or C: Holland?

John Well, I (**6**) **wouldn't / won't** be confident if I chose B. And C is silly …

Frankie I need (**7**) **having / to have** an answer …

John OK, Frankie. I've decided (**8**) **choosing / to choose** A.

Frankie Well, John … you're wrong! The answer is C: Holland!

Culture focus

1 **Do the culture quiz. Look for the answers in your Student's Book and Workbook if necessary.**

Section A   Find the odd one out.
(1 point for each correct answer)

1 Which one is not a language?

   a Esperanto ☐

   b Maluerindi ☐

   c Norse ☐

2 Which one is not an African animal?

   a cheetah ☐

   b antelope ☐

   c baobab ☐

3 Which one is not the name of an island?

   a Kyoto ☐

   b Kefalonia ☐

   c Kiribati ☐

4 Which one does not create CO_2 (carbon dioxide)?

   a Burning petrol ☐

   b Burning vegetable oil ☐

   c Burning coal ☐

5 Which one is not a group of people?

   a Makuleke ☐

   b Sioux ☐

   c Uluru ☐

6 Which one is not a national park?

   a Black Hills ☐

   b Kruger ☐

   c Kata Tjuta ☐

Section B Answer the questions.
(3 points for each correct answer)

1 Who was Crazy Horse?

_____

2 Why was there a big vibration in the Australian desert in 1993?

_____

3 What colour is the anti-bullying wristband?

_____

4 Which large black cat have people seen in Scotland?

_____

5 What did Ludovic Zamenhof invent?

_____

6 How many people will there be on Earth by 2030?

_____

7 How much would you win if you invented an 'intelligent' talking robot?

_____

8 How many languages are there in the world?

_____

Your score?   **/ 30**

7 Times of change

Reading

1 Read the text quickly. What is special about the dog in the photo? _____

Snuppy

A [3] Every year, some truly astonishing things are invented. Some technological inventions, especially, are incredible. So it was a surprise when, in 2005, *Time Magazine* announced that a dog was the winner of its annual 'Invention of the Year' award. But not just any old dog. The year's best invention was a dog called Snuppy. Although he is a normal, healthy dog, his origins are definitely not normal: Snuppy is a 'clone'.

B [ ] Snuppy was not produced in a normal way by two parent dogs. Instead, he was created by scientists. They copied DNA from his father and put the DNA inside his mother. Then he was born in the normal way.

C [ ] People have enjoyed pets for thousands of years. Keeping cats, dogs and fish is normal. But what about making a copy of your pet – is that normal? Many people do not see a problem with copying nature. These days, if you have a lot of money, you can select a type of cat, its colour and even the colour of its eyes, and scientists can make it.

In the future, it may even be possible to create animals that do not get ill. Some people think that this is great news, but a lot of people disagree. They believe that it is very wrong to interfere with nature.

D [ ] According to scientists, cloning is used to help find cures for human diseases. However, opponents of cloning say that the technology is unsafe. For example, cloned animals often have health problems. The first animal that was cloned was a sheep. Dolly the sheep was created in a laboratory in Scotland in 1996. She died of a disease before her seventh birthday. This is a common problem with cloned animals.

E [ ] This debate will continue for many years. But, at least for the moment, everyone feels the same about one important thing: it is wrong to make copies of people.

2 Match the headings 1–5 with the paragraphs A–E.

1 Copycats
2 Is cloning safe?
3 Invention of the Year
4 No human clones
5 What is cloning?

3 Answer the questions. Use full sentences.

Who organises a competition for inventions every year?
'Time Magazine' organises 'Invention of the Year'.

1 Who created Snuppy, and how?
_____

2 What choices can rich people make about a pet?
_____

3 How do some scientists think that cloning can help people?
_____

4 What is one disadvantage of cloning?
_____

5 What do supporters and critics of cloning agree on?
_____

Grammar

Passive

1 Underline the verb forms. Tick ✓ the passive sentences.

Hundreds of new games <u>are invented</u> every year. ✓

1 Some inventions are incredible. ☐

2 Is much money given to inventors? ☐

3 When is the winner announced? ☐

4 Scientific research is expensive. ☐

5 Are they happy about the situation? ☐

6 The award is given to the best invention. ☐

7 This is not an unusual situation. ☐

8 The results of the tests are not known yet. ☐

Present simple passive

2 Complete the sentences with the present simple passive form of the verbs in brackets.

Most American films *are produced* (produce) in Hollywood.

1 Paper _____ (make) from wood.

2 _____ beef _____ (eat) in India?

3 Euros _____ (not use) in all European countries.

4 _____ rice _____ (grow) in Thailand?

5 _____ English _____ (speak) in China?

6 Letters _____ (not deliver) on holidays.

7 Thanksgiving Day _____ (not celebrate) in our country.

8 _____ football _____ (play) in the USA?

3 Rewrite the active sentences in the present simple passive. (You do not need to say who does the action.)

They test every type of new food.
Every type of new food is tested.

1 Scientists make amazing discoveries every year.
_____

2 Do you accept credit cards in this shop?
_____

3 Shops don't sell video recorders very often.
_____

4 Do they produce Porsche cars in America?
_____

5 Chefs do not invent new recipes every day.
_____

6 Do you sell the new 2.5 GHz laptop here?
_____

Past simple passive

4 Write sentences in the past simple passive.

the first ballpoint pen / produce / Lazslo Biro / 1938
The ballpoint pen was produced by Lazslo Biro in 1938.

1 the computer mouse / not invent / until 1964
_____
_____

2 when / the first CD / play / ?
_____

3 bicycles / not use / before the nineteenth century
_____
_____

4 the first tyre without air (the Tweel) / drive / in 2005
_____
_____

5 Rewrite the active sentences in the past simple passive. (You do not need to say who did the action.)

They cooked an enormous pizza in New York last year.
An enormous pizza was cooked in New York last year.

1 Did he publish his first book in 1997?

_____

2 They didn't leave the door open.

_____

3 They cleaned the kitchen quite well.

_____

4 They invented credit cards in 1950.

_____

5 When did they produce the first colour TV?

_____

6 Biologists discovered a new species of mammal.

_____

6 Complete the sentences with the present or past simple passive form of the verbs in brackets.

Which currency *was used* (use) in France before the euro?

1 Cheese _____ (produce) in many countries.

2 Esperanto _____ (not speak) in 1850.

3 _____ coffee _____ (serve) here after ten o'clock?

4 Oranges _____ (not grow) in Scotland.

5 _____ Arabic _____ (speak) in Spain 1,500 years ago?

6 The first record _____ (play) in 1889.

7 Complete each active sentence so that it means the same as the passive sentence.

Were they arrested yesterday?
Did the police *arrest them yesterday*?

1 These pictures were painted by Picasso.
Picasso _____.

2 Is English spoken in Ireland?
Do they _____?

3 Extra marks are given for presentation.
Teachers _____.

4 That website is visited by thousands of people every day.
Thousands of people _____.

Consolidation

8 Complete the text with the active, present passive or past passive form of the verbs in brackets.

The $100 laptop
The 'digital divide' between the rich and developing countries of the world *was made* (make) smaller recently, when the MIT Media Lab _____ (1 announce) a new sub-$100 laptop. MIT _____ (2 come up with) the idea as part of their One Laptop Per Child (OLPC) project. OLPC's laptops _____ (3 give) to children in developing countries so that they can have a better education. Before OLPC, not many computers _____ (4 sell) in developing countries. Now millions will have internet access.

The laptop _____ (5 not sell) in shops. Instead, it _____ (6 distribute) to schools by ministries of education. The laptop _____ (7 make) from cheap but good, strong materials. The most important thing is that it _____ (8 not use) electricity. Instead, power _____ (9 generate) with a handle on the side of the laptop. Often there is no telephone line either, so the laptops _____ (10 connect) to the internet via a mobile phone.

Communication

Vocabulary Phrasal verbs

1 Rewrite the sentences with the correct form of the verbs in the box.

> call off ~~come across~~ come up with
> give up keep on put up with sort out

> By chance, I found these old photos under my bed.
> *I came across these old photos under my bed.*

1 I don't know how you tolerate him.

   _____

2 My mum has stopped smoking.

   _____

3 They invented a mobile with a radar inside.

   _____

4 The picnic was cancelled.

   _____

5 My dad is tidying the garage.

   _____

6 I want to continue learning English.

   _____

Human achievement

2 Complete the sentences with the correct noun form of the verbs in brackets.

> The plane was a great *development* (develop) in transport.

1 What was the most significant _____ (discover) of the twentieth century?

2 Scientific _____ (research) is very important.

3 Who was the _____ (invent) of the internet?

4 Space _____ (explore) are expensive but they help us to understand Earth.

5 _____ (research) are doing very important work to help us understand global warming.

6 My dad comes up with some amazing ideas for _____ (invent), but they never work!

Extension MATERIALS

3 Label the pictures with the nouns in the box.

> concrete ~~fabric~~ glass leather metal plastic
> rubber wood

fabric   1 _____   2 _____   3 _____

4 _____   5 _____   6 _____   7 _____

4 Which materials are they made from? Use the nouns from exercise 3.

> mobile phone: *metal, plastic*

1 bicycle: _____

2 trainers: _____

3 jacket: _____

4 table: _____

5 tin-opener: _____

Speaking Short answers

5 Complete the dialogue with the phrases in the box.

> Yes, it is.   No, it isn't.   Yes, they are.
> ~~No, they aren't.~~   Yes, you can.   No, you can't.

Amy Are they found outside?

Carl *No, they aren't.*

Amy Are they found in a house?

Carl (1) _____. Usually only one.

Amy Is it made from glass?

Carl (2) _____.

Amy Is it made from fabric?

Carl (3) _____. Well, part of it.

Amy Ah! Can you wear it?

Carl (4) _____.

Amy Can you sleep on it?

Carl (5) _____. If you want!

Amy I know what it is! Is it a …?

Writing

A discussion essay

Expressions for introducing, adding and contrasting

1 Choose the best expressions in the box to complete the sentences.

> also   however   in addition   ~~on the other hand~~
> on the one hand   such as   this means that

You should take up IT classes. *On the other hand*, you could call me every time your laptop breaks!

1 This laptop copies CDs. It _____ copies DVDs.

2 This program is used by experts _____ web designers.

3 Some people are afraid of new things. _____ inventions are often unpopular at first.

4 These monitors aren't made in this country. _____, they are imported quite cheaply.

2 Match the sentences 1–6 with the spaces A–F in the essay in exercise 3.

1 For example, robots are used at the moment for doing specific jobs.

2 However, we need to be cautious with technology.

3 In conclusion, there are benefits from having intelligent robots.

4 On the one hand, some people love technology.

5 On the other hand, some people worry that technology could also bring problems.

6 This means that our health may suffer because we will be less active.

3 Read the essay again and tick ✓ the best title.

1 We must develop our technology more. Discuss. ☐

2 We should develop better robots. Discuss. ☐

3 Robots are unnecessary these days. Discuss. ☐

> **(A)** 4 They want to keep up with technological developments, so they are worried that robots are not used enough. **(B)** ☐ They are good at things such as housework or building cars. However, it is possible to develop robots that can do many more jobs which can save us time, energy and money.
>
> **(C)** ☐ Robots might help us, but they would also make us lazier. If robots were more intelligent, they would do more jobs for us. **(D)** ☐ In addition, if robots were cleverer, they would be able to do more complex jobs, but would robots become too clever? If robots could 'think', would they also control us?
>
> **(E)** ☐ They would make our lives easier. **(F)** ☐

4 Write two conclusions. Use *in conclusion*, *however* and the words in the box.

> they are expensive   ~~cars give us great mobility~~
> microwaves save a lot of time
> it is also healthier to eat fresh food
> in addition, they create too much carbon dioxide
> they make us lazy and we do not learn how to cook

1 Everyone should drive a car. Discuss.
In conclusion, cars give us great mobility. However, _____
_____
_____

2 Microwaves mean poor health. Discuss.
_____
_____
_____
_____
_____
_____

Vocabulary

1 Complete the sentences with the correct form of the phrasal verbs in the box.

> call off   come across   find out   give up
> keep up   make up   put up with   sort out

1 I can't _____. Don't run so quickly!
2 How do they _____ their noisy neighbours?
3 I don't believe it. Her story is _____.
4 Did the detectives _____ about it?
5 The concert was _____.
6 I'm going to _____ my bedroom this weekend.
7 My dad _____ eating chocolates last year.
8 Did you _____ any interesting websites?

2 Complete the text with words for human achievement.

A (1) r_____ at Bath University has (2) i_____ a new method of reducing air pollution. Her (3) i_____ is the result of a lucky (4) d_____, followed by three years of hard work. After this long period of (5) d_____, the (6) i_____ of the technique wants a holiday!

Vocabulary review: Units 1–7

3 Choose the correct answers.

1 I **had** / **felt** a cold and a **sore** / **sprain** throat.
2 'When are they going to **carry out** / **realise** the experiment?'
   'I don't know, but we hope that it will be a **success** / **an exit**.'
3 They **say** / **tell** that **making** / **getting** money is easy.
4 **Greenhouse** / **Global** warming occurs when you **burn** / **grow** oil.
5 He's **reliable** / **decisive**. He always **remembers** / **records** to call.

Grammar

4 Write sentences in the present simple passive.

1 Ferraris / not make / in the UK
   _____
2 Italian / speak / in Italy
   _____
3 Cheese / produce / in France / ?
   _____
4 that book / not translate / into English
   _____

5 Rewrite the active sentences in the past simple passive. (You do not need to say who did the action.)

1 They didn't record this DVD for you.
   _____
2 I didn't write that song this year.
   _____
3 We used the peseta for years.
   _____
4 They produced the film in Zaragoza.
   _____

Grammar review: Units 1–7

6 Complete the text with the words in the box.

> are made   going to have   have invented   have to
> if   is felt   may be   moves   to change   wearing

Scientists (1) _____ 'faster clothes'

During training, athletes normally (2) _____ listen to their coach's advice. But it takes time for the athlete to respond. However, (3) _____ 'faster clothes' helps athletes (4) _____ the way that they are training very quickly. How? Faster clothes (5) _____ with electronic sensors. These detect the movement of the athlete's body. If the wearer (6) _____ too quickly or too slowly, the clothes vibrate. This (7) _____ immediately and the athlete can vary his or her training.

This (8) _____ great news for athletes, but some coaches are worried. 'Are we (9) _____ a job in five years?' asked one coach. 'What will we do (10) _____ faster clothes take our work?'

8 | Achievement

Reading

High flyer

A daring young Oxford man has achieved his ambition of running his own business – when he was only eighteen. Martin Halstead lives with his mother, who still cannot believe that her son owns an airline. 'Age is just a number,' says Mr Halstead.

A childhood dream

Mr Halstead, now nineteen, had been obsessed with flying since his first flight, at the age of six. Although he was hard-working at school, he left after his GCSEs to focus on a career. It was then that Mr Halstead decided to start his own airline, AlphaOne.

Universities united

It takes three hours to travel the 190 km by road between the English university cities of Oxford and Cambridge. There was a direct train service until 1967, but these days you have to travel via London and change trains. Mr Halstead was looking at a map when he noticed that the actual distance between the two cities is only 100 km. Then he realised that an air service could make a major difference to this inconvenient journey. And since then, his phone has not stopped ringing.

Friends in high places

One of these callers was Sir Richard Branson. Sir Richard lives near Oxford and he owns at the age of one of the most successful airlines in the world. Branson is enthusiastic about AlphaOne and he has given Mr Halstead a lot of advice. The friendship has been an inspiration to Mr Halstead, and has earnt him the nickname 'baby Branson'. 'But I don't want to be the next Richard Branson,' he said. 'I want to be the first Martin Halstead.'

Try and try again

There have been some very difficult times, but Halstead is determined, and success does not always come easily. After all, if it was easy to start a business, everyone would do it! In 2005, he abandoned his plans to fly from Oxford to Cambridge, but he did not abandon his dream. He bought a new plane, found more pilots and began flying various routes from the Isle of Man, an island between Ireland and the UK, to Southampton in England, Cardiff in Wales and Edinburgh in Scotland.

AlphaOne started small, but it is growing fast. Have you booked your seat?

---

1 Read the text. Are the sentences true or false? Explain your answers.

> Mrs Halstead is surprised that Martin is a businessman.
> *True. Martin's mother cannot believe it.*

1 Martin Halstead studied business at university.

_____

2 A road journey from Oxford to Cambridge is almost twice as far as a flight.

_____

3 Richard Branson has lent Halstead a lot of money.

_____

4 Halstead is copying Richard Branson.

_____

2 Read the text again and answer the questions.

> What is Martin Halstead's passion?
> *He has always wanted to have his own business.*

1 When did Halstead first travel by plane?

_____

2 What is the problem with the Oxford–Cambridge train service?

_____

3 How did Halstead come up with the idea of flying between Oxford and Cambridge?

_____

4 Does AlphaOne fly to Ireland?

_____

Grammar

Relative clauses

1 Match 1–7 with a–g to make sentences.

1 She's the actress   `c`
2 Is he the businessman ☐
3 I don't like people ☐
4 Will the film be ready ☐
5 Can you remember ☐
6 That's the school ☐
7 This isn't the film ☐

a that give up easily.
b when Angelina gets back?
c who I most admire.
d where I sat my GCSEs.
e which translation you read?
f that we wanted to watch.
g whose companies are for sale?

2 Match the relative pronouns 1–6 with the uses a–f. Then check your answers in exercise 1.

1 that   `b`
2 when ☐
3 where ☐
4 which ☐
5 who ☐
6 whose ☐

a person
b person or thing
c of a person (possessive)
d place
e thing
f time

Defining clauses
that, which and *who*

3 Write sentences with relative clauses.

I lent / the book / that / have you got / to you / ?
Have you got the book that I lent to you?

1 presented sports programmes / she / who / 's / the TV star

_____

2 the CD / that / is / that / want to buy / I

_____

3 that / where / you / is / the present / bought / ?

_____

4 which / the film / hasn't seen / you / he / like

_____

5 anyone / who / I / don't know / play the guitar / can

_____

4 Complete the sentences with *who* or *which*. Then cross (X) the sentences in which the relative pronouns are not necessary.

We've got a music teacher *who* plays the drums. ☐

1 No, I haven't seen the girl _____ you like! ☐
2 Do you know anyone _____ can ski? ☐
3 I don't like singers _____ sing in English. ☐
4 Is this the CD _____ you wanted? ☐
5 No one wants friends _____ are mean. ☐
6 That isn't the player _____ I'm thinking of. ☐
7 PE is the only class _____ I hate! ☐
8 Ambition is a quality _____ I admire. ☐

Defining clauses
where, when and *whose*

5 Complete the text with *where, when* or *whose*.

I go to a school *where* there's no uniform. This may sound great, but there are disadvantages to the system.

It means that we can choose our clothes in nice shops (1) _____ they sell other things like earrings and make-up. The girls at other schools have to go to a shop (2) _____ they only sell uniform and it's really boring!

However, there are times (3) _____ some girls (4) _____ parents are richer wear really expensive things at school, and their clothes are nicer than ours. That's why I'd prefer a school (5) _____ there is a uniform.

6 Write relative clauses with *where*, *when* or *whose*.

This is the primary school. I studied here three years ago.
This is the primary school where I studied three years ago.

1 I remember the day. I started school.

_____

_____

2 She's the girl. Her mother is an actress.

_____

_____

3 I don't like winter days. It gets dark very early.

_____

_____

4 That's the shop. They sell excellent ice-cream.

_____

_____

5 Those are the boys. Their father works at the library.

_____

_____

whose or *who's?*

7 Complete the sentences with *whose* or *who's*.
Where the answer is *who's*, write *who is* or *who has*.

My best friend is a person ...

who's (= who is) really reliable.

1 _____ come through life's problems with me.

2 _____ enthusiasm I admire.

3 _____ never jealous.

4 _____ ideas I love.

5 _____ trustworthy.

6 _____ secrets I understand.

Consolidation

8 Complete the text with the words in the box. There is sometimes more than one answer.

| that which where when who who's whose |

Meet the Mayor

Meet the man (**1**) _____ just won control of Hillsdale, Michigan, USA. In the year (**2**) _____ he became eighteen, Michael Sessions also became Mayor of Hillsdale in the local elections.

From eight a.m. until two-thirty p.m., Mr Sessions will go to the high school (**3**) _____ he is still a student. Then, from three until six p.m., he will do all the things (**4**) _____ a mayor has to do. And from six p.m., he will do the homework (**5**) _____ he has to do every day. Everybody (**6**) _____ goes to Hillsdale High School has to do their homework, although many have a part-time job as well.

'We have students (**7**) _____ work at Burger King,' explains the principal. 'There are others (**8**) _____ parents buy their clothes and everything for them. And we have one (**9**) _____ going to work in the Mayor's office. We're proud to have a student (**10**) _____ ambition is to improve this town. But homework is homework.'

Communication

Vocabulary Success

1 Complete the sentences with one of each pair of words in the box.

> enthusiastic / enthusiasm   luck / lucky
> resource / resourceful   ~~skilful / skill~~
> success / successful

You need a lot of *skill* to fly a helicopter.

1 Mary is very excited and _____ about this project.
2 I don't believe in bad _____ .
3 _____ people always find a way of doing things.
4 I've worked hard but I haven't had much _____ yet.

-ed and -ing adjectives

2 Complete the text with the correct form of the adjectives.

Becky What's wrong? You look really frustrat*ed*.
Steve Oh, I'm just **(1)** annoy_____. Every time I try to start my moped, there's a **(2)** disgus_____ smell of petrol. Mopeds are so **(3)** frustrat_____!
Becky Well, it's better than being **(4)** bor_____ at home, isn't it?
Steve I suppose so. The **(5)** embarrass_____ thing is that my friends laugh at me.
Becky Why don't you fix it, then?
Steve The engine's really **(6)** confus_____. And I feel **(7)** embarrass_____ that I can't fix it. I feel **(8)** annoy_____ too.
Becky Here, I'll call you a taxi.

Extension ADVERBS

3 Complete the sentences with the adverbs in the wordsquare.

> *Luckily* (lucky), I remembered to call him.

1 He played the violin very _____ (skilful).
2 This coffee is _____ (disgusting) sweet.
3 He acted that part quite _____ (amusing).
4 They have _____ (successful) made three films.
5 Why are TV adverts always _____ (annoying) loud?
6 *Starmaker* _____ (proud) presents … Kylie!

D	I	S	G	U	S	T	I	N	G	L	Y	L	Y
A	M	S	U	C	C	E	S	S	F	U	L	L	Y
S	A	M	U	S	I	N	G	L	Y	C	O	O	L
A	S	K	I	L	F	U	L	L	Y	K	I	N	G
I	M	P	R	O	U	D	L	Y	O	I	L	G	Y
D	R	A	N	N	O	Y	I	N	G	L	Y	T	S
Y	S	A	O	C	S	Y	E	G	R	Y	L	R	Y

Speaking Ways of speaking

4 Match the sentences with the words in the box. Where or when might you say each sentence?

> angrily   ~~cheerfully~~   confidently   loudly
> nervously   quietly

Good morning! How are you? *cheerfully*
When you see someone in the morning.

1 Come on, Liverpool! Liverpool! Liverpool!
   _____
   _____

2 Now the film has started, we can't talk.
   _____
   _____

3 Please, Miss! I know the answer. _____
   _____

4 Oh, no! I hate it when I miss an easy goal!
   _____
   _____

5 I've never taken part in a competition before.
   _____
   _____

Writing

A book review
Informal descriptions

1 Read the extracts from a book review and match paragraphs A–D with 1–4. Then read the review in the correct order, 1–4.

1 the setting   [c]
2 the characters   [ ]
3 the plot   [ ]
4 highlights   [ ]

B

The detectives and the policeman decide to wait in the cellar. (3) _____ . Eventually the criminals come out of the tunnel and they are arrested.

C

I have just read *The Red-headed League*. (4) _____ and his friend Dr Watson, but it is more amusing than most of the stories, and nobody is killed. Indeed, rather than solving a crime after it has been committed, the two friends actually catch the criminals at work.

A

A shopkeeper comes to visit Sherlock and explains that a man is paying him a lot of money to work in an office a long way from his shop, on the other side of London. (1) The situation is extremely suspicious. After some time, Sherlock realises that a clever criminal, John Clay, has dug a tunnel from a shop to the cellar of a bank. Sherlock is a very intelligent detective. (2) _____ . The cellar is full of gold.

D

As well as Sherlock and Dr Watson, we meet Mr Jabez Wilson, a shopkeeper who helps them. There is also a police detective, Mr Jones, who helps Sherlock. The police do not usually work so closely with him.

★★★★★ **Marie Brown**, Birmingham

2 Match 1–8 with a–h to make sentences.

1 The situation is   [e]
2 The time they spend waiting [ ]
3 I almost   [ ]
4 It's another exciting story [ ]
5 His powers of deduction   [ ]
6 I couldn't   [ ]

a a nail-biting climax.
b are quite remarkable.
c fell asleep.
d stop yawning.
e extremely suspicious.
f involving Sherlock Holmes

3 Complete the spaces 1–4 in the review with expressions from exercise 2.

4 Which two expressions did you not use in exercise 2? Why are they not used?

1 _____

2 _____

5 Read the review again. How is this story different to other Sherlock Holmes stories that the reviewer has read?

1 _____
2 _____
3 _____

Quick check

Vocabulary

1 Complete the sentences with the noun forms of the adjectives for success in the box.

> ambitious   determined   enthusiastic
> hard-working   self-confident   talented

Tim   His (1) a_____ was to give up work before he was 40.

Pat   Really? Where did he get that amazing (2) d_____? I mean, his (3) e_____ for all that (4) h_____ is extraordinary.

Tim   His (5) s_____ comes from his father's family. The creative (6) t_____ must be from his mother's side.

2 Choose the correct *-ed* or *-ing* form.

1   It's **embarrassed / embarrassing**. I've forgotten his name.
2   This DVD is really **shocked / shocking**.
3   Everyone on the beach was **annoyed / annoying** by the dog.
4   Beefburgers are **disgusted / disgusting**!
5   What an **amused / amusing** story!
6   Waiting for buses can be **frustrated / frustrating**.
7   I'm really **confused / confusing** by phrasal verbs.
8   What's wrong? Are you **bored / boring**?

Vocabulary review: Units 1–8

3 Complete the text with the words in the box.

> come through   determination   explorers
> fearless   freezing   keep on   luck   storms

Arctic (1) _____ are (2) _____ people. They (3) _____ walking for many hours in (4) _____ snow and ice, and severe (5) _____. Their incredible (6) _____ helps them to (7) _____ difficult situations. Some say that they must be lucky; others say that they make their own (8) _____.

Grammar

4 Match 1–6 with a–f to make sentences. Then complete the sentences with the relative pronouns in the box. There is sometimes more than one answer.

> that   when   where   which   who   whose

1   Do you remember the house ☐
2   We need a coach ☐
3   Where's the CD ☐
4   Is that the time ☐
5   I need some boots ☐
6   This is my dad's friend ☐

a   _____ we cycled to London?
b   _____ car we borrowed.
c   _____ knows how to win.
d   _____ you lived ten years ago?
e   _____ are waterproof.
f   _____ Frank lent us?

Grammar review: Units 1–8

5 Complete the text with the words in the box.

> not used   is going to give   giving
> has announced   seeing   to die   to help
> which   who   would go

The woman (1) _____ founded the Body Shop, Anita Roddick, (2) _____ that she (3) _____ her £50 million (€75 million) fortune to charity. If Ms Roddick kept her fortune, all the money (4) _____ to the government in taxes after her death. If a rich person's money is (5) _____ while they are alive, it cannot help others, and, as Anita explained, 'I don't want (6) _____ rich.' (7) _____ money to charity means that rich people can enjoy (8) _____ how their donation helps others. But with 180,000 charities in the UK, the hard part is deciding which charity you want (9) _____. Experts predict that Ms Roddick will donate to charities (10) _____ work on human rights issues.

9 | Off to see the world

Reading

1 Read the text quickly. What is the 'long way round'? _____

Long way round

A Ewan McGregor is one of the most famous actors in the world. His best friend is the actor Charley Boorman. McGregor and Boorman share two things in life: their profession and their passion for motorcycling. After many long conversations about bike trips, they finally made a plan to ride around the world on two wheels. This would be the trip of their lives.

B They planned a route from London to New York – via Asia (Ukraine, Russia, Kazakhstan and Mongolia). In other words, not across the Atlantic, but the 'long way round'. The roads were dangerous and hundreds of kilometres from civilisation, so they spent months learning about survival, first aid and motorcycle mechanics.

C They eventually left London in April 2004 on bikes which were heavy with luggage. A cameraman rode with them on another bike because they wanted to film the journey.

D The roads in Europe, Canada and the USA were fine, but some of the roads in Asia were awful. Some of the roads in Mongolia were terrifying. Their bikes broke again and again, but they fixed the bikes and kept on riding. After a while, they loved Mongolia. The scenery was incredibly beautiful and the Mongolians were the friendliest people that they met on their whole journey.

E In Siberia (Russia), they had to cross deep, extremely cold rivers on their bikes. They were freezing and the heavy bikes were exhausting. McGregor said that they had wanted to give up but that they had been determined to succeed.

F In the end, their epic 30,000 km journey took four months. They said that they were proud because they had stayed on their motorcycles for most of the way, apart from a 1,000 km train journey in an area without roads in Siberia. They also took a plane from Siberia across the Bering Sea to Alaska (USA).

G McGregor said that their dreams had come true. He said that it had been very tough and that it really had been a 'long way round'. Their journey has become a best-selling book and TV series, both called *Long Way Round*.

2 Tick ✓ the best alternative title.

1 Two wheels across continents ☐
2 Around the world in 80 days ☐
3 Two wheels around America ☐

3 Answer the questions. Use full sentences.

What two things do McGregor and Boorman have in common?
They are both actors and they love motorbikes.

1 Why did they study motorcycle mechanics?
_____

2 How many riders left London on the journey?
_____

3 Why was Mongolia a country of contrasts?
_____
_____

4 How did they feel in Siberia?
_____

5 What were they pleased about when they had finished?
_____
_____

6 Which parts of the journey did they not do on motorbikes, and why?
_____

7 How can you find out more about their journey?
_____

Grammar

Reported speech

1 Match the direct statements 1–6 with the reported statements a–f.

1 'I'll ride a moped.'　　　　　　　　　　 `d`
2 'I have ridden a moped.'　　　　　　 ☐
3 'I can ride a moped.'　　　　　　　　 ☐
4 'I didn't ride a moped.'　　　　　　　 ☐
5 'I ride a moped.'　　　　　　　　　　 ☐
6 'I'm riding a moped.'　　　　　　　　 ☐

I said that I …

a could ride a moped.
b was riding a moped.
c hadn't ridden a moped.
d would ride a moped.
e rode a moped.
f had ridden a moped.

2 Choose the correct forms in the box to complete the reported statements.

> will be   won't be   ~~would be~~   wouldn't be
> hadn't caught   haven't caught   is catching
> was catching   disappeared   had disappeared
> can't hear   couldn't hear   hadn't left   hasn't left

'We'll be there at six.'
She said that they _would be_ there at six.

1 'They didn't catch the bus at nine.'
He said that they _____ the bus at nine.

2 'I won't be late.'
She said that she _____ late.

3 'I'm catching the five o'clock bus.'
She said that she _____ the five o'clock bus.

4 'John hadn't left a message.'
She said that John _____ a message.

5 'I can't hear you.'
He said that he _____ me.

6 'You've disappeared.'
She said that he _____.

3 Complete the reported statements. Change the pronouns and the verb tenses.

'I want to go to China,' said Charley.
Charley said that _he wanted_ to go to China.

1 'We can't go across that river,' said Ewan.
Ewan said that _____ _____ _____ across that river.

2 'I'm filming you!' said the cameraman.
The cameraman said that _____ _____ _____ them.

3 'We didn't get permission to enter Tibet,' said the producer.
The producer said that _____ _____ _____ permission to enter Tibet.

4 'We haven't bought enough petrol,' said Ewan.
Ewan said that _____ _____ _____ enough petrol.

5 'I won't sleep there!' said Charley.
Charley said that _____ _____ there.

4 Put the words in order to make reported statements.

said / in a tent again. / that / Ewan / didn't want / he / to sleep
Ewan said that he didn't want to sleep in a tent again.

1 was / it / freezing outside. / that / the cameraman / said

_____
_____

2 that / Siberia before. / Charley / had never visited / said / he

_____
_____

3 he / hadn't wanted / to ride so far. / said / Ewan / that

_____
_____

4 Charley / he / problems with his bike. / that / was having / said

_____
_____

5 **Report the statements.**

Deb Graham's invited us to a picnic. It'll be really good.

Deb said that Graham had invited them to a picnic.
She said that it would be really good.

1 Rob Philippa doesn't work there any more. She's changed jobs.

Rob _____

_____

He _____

2 Cathy Hannah's got a new computer. She's really happy.

Cathy _____

_____

She _____

_____

3 Neil I'm leaving soon. I haven't made any new plans.

Neil _____

He _____

_____

4 Gordon Tony has made too many mistakes. He's making our problems worse.

Gordon _____

_____

He _____

_____

say or *tell*?

6 **Complete the sentences with *said* or *told*.**

He *said* that he was getting on at King's Cross.

1 Philip _____ me that he had forgotten to get off.

2 She _____ her husband that she was cooking.

3 We _____ that we wanted to cycle.

4 The bus driver _____ that we had missed our stop.

5 I _____ them that I was parking the car.

6 The teacher _____ us that we could catch a bus.

Consolidation

7 **Report the dialogue between Rob and Fiona. Use *said* and *told*.**

Rob I'm going to read you an article from my magazine. It's an amazing story!

1 Fiona I'm reading. You can tell me later.

2 Rob It's only short.

3 Fiona I'm listening.

4 Rob 'A Chinese farmer is taking a message of peace around the world. In ten months, he has ridden his old motorbike from China to Africa.'

5 Fiona I don't believe you!

6 Rob It's true. 'He has visited every Asian country and most of Africa's 53 countries. He is going to take his message of peace to every country in the world.'

Rob told Fiona that he was going to read her an article from his magazine. He said that it was an amazing story.

_____

_____

_____

_____

_____

_____

_____

_____

_____

_____

_____

_____

_____

_____

_____

Communication

Vocabulary Travel (1)

1 Match 1–5 with a–e to make sentences.

1 We went on a different   `d`
2 Travel is now   ☐
3 They've gone on a skiing   ☐
4 The quickest way is a   ☐
5 Thirty-six hours is a   ☐

a flight from Paris to London.
b long journey.
c the world's biggest industry.
d tour every day.
e trip to Switzerland.

2 Complete the text with the words in the box.

> bus ~~caught~~ got out got into got off got on
> missed take taxi train

I caught the (1) _____ in my street at
8.00 and (2) _____ at the station. I decided
to (3) _____ the fast train to Paddington.
Unfortunately, I had (4) _____ the 8.20
(5) _____, so I (6) _____
the 8.45 and arrived in Paddington at 10.00.

I was in a hurry, so I had to take a (7) _____.
I (8) _____ the first one that I saw.
The driver said that it would be £12, so I checked my
cash but somebody had stolen my wallet! I couldn't
pay, so I (9) _____ and found a policeman.

Travel (2)

3 Find the words in brackets. Complete the text.

Passengers (g e r s s p a s e n) catch trains at a
_____ (1 s a n t i t o). You can buy
your _____ (2 t e t i c k) online,
from a machine or at the _____
(3 c i k t e t f o c e f i). Then you listen to the
_____ (4 c a n e n e m u t s n n o)
to find out which _____
(5 p o l m r a f t) you need. Sometimes you have to get
into the correct _____ (6 r a g e c r i a)
and this information is also on the ticket.

Extension MOPEDS

4 Find seven words in the wordsquare. Label the picture.

W	E	B	R	A	K	E	R	S	U	E	P
H	E	L	Z	P	L	R	O	A	D	U	O
E	N	I	S	M	Z	O	P	D	O	D	H
E	G	G	Y	R	L	M	O	D	S	S	A
L	I	H	S	T	E	D	I	L	F	F	L
E	N	T	H	A	N	D	L	E	B	A	R
G	E	T	H	R	O	T	T	L	E	D	Y

1 throttle
2 s _ _ _ _ e
3 e _ _ _ _ e
4 w _ _ _ l
5 b _ _ _ e
6 l _ _ _ t
7 h _ _ _ _ _ _ r

Speaking Learning to ride

5 Complete the dialogue with the words in the box.

> accelerate hold ~~put on~~ pull sit

Pete It's easy. First, put on this helmet. Then
        (1) _____ here, on the saddle.
Sam I'll fall over!
Pete No, you won't. I'll (2) _____ on to
        the handlebar. Now, you (3) _____
        with the throttle, here.
Sam OK. And how do I stop?
Pete To stop, (4) _____ this. This is
        the brake. And remember: always use
        your front brake before the back brake.

Writing

A formal letter Parts of a letter

1 Complete parts 1, 2, 3 and 7 of the letter with a–d.

a
31st April 2007

b
Ms Harriet Waters
Cyclox
28 East Avenue
Oxford
OX1 4XP

c
Thomas Cox
Thomas Cox

d
28A Dean Square
Camberwell
London E17

1 _____
  _____
  _____
2 _____

3 _____
  _____
  _____
  _____
  _____

4 _____
5 _____
  _____
  _____
  _____
  _____
  _____
  _____
  _____
  _____
  _____
  _____
  _____
  _____
  _____

6 _____
7 _____
  _____

2 Choose the correct opening greeting in the box to complete part 4.

Dear Mr Cox   Dear Harriet
Dear Harriet Waters   Dear Ms Waters
Dear Sir or Madam   Dear Thomas

3 Choose the correct closing greeting in the box to complete part 6.

Yours attentively   Yours faithfully
Yours patiently   Yours sincerely

Formal language

4 Choose the correct formal sentences in a–c to complete part 5.

a I am writing about your advertisement in *Summer Holidays* magazine for seven-day bicycle tours.
   I read your advert in *Summer Holidays* and I'm writing to ask about the 7-day bike tours.

b Could you tell me the minimum age for going on the rides?
   What is the minimum age for going on the rides?

c I read that the tours leave on Saturdays in June and July, but can you send me more details about the tours, please?
   Your advertisement said that the rides left every Saturday in June and July. I would be grateful if you could send me some more details about the tours.

Quick check

Vocabulary

1 **Choose the correct answer.**

1 We went on a **travel** / **trip** to Mexico.
2 The **journey** / **travel** to the mountains is easy.
3 **Travel** / **flight** gets more popular every year.
4 The **journey** / **tour** of the museum starts at four.

2 **Complete the sentences with travel words. Use the past simple form of the verbs.**

1 We c_____ our plane at the
   a_____.
2 He t_____ the number 74 bus to the
   train s_____.
3 We g_____ i_____ the car
   and d_____ home.
4 My little sister r_____ a bike for the first
   time yesterday!
5 We m_____ the 10.00 bus but we
   g_____ o_____ the number
   14 at 10.30.
6 Did you remember to take your bags when you
   g_____ o_____
   o_____ the taxi?
7 They g_____ o_____ the
   plane in Hong Kong on the way to Sydney.
8 My brother can't remember where he p_____
   his car!

Vocabulary review: Units 1–9

3 **<u>Underline</u> the word which is the most different in each group.**

1 platform   gate   runway   announcement
2 breeze   gentle   severe   strong
3 discovery   resource   exploration   researcher
4 rise   expand   grow   reduce
5 chin   thigh   ankle   toe
6 nervous   anxious   daring   cautious
7 memorise   practice   repeat   translate
8 fantastic   terrifying   astonishing   thrilling

Grammar

4 **Report these statements.**

1 Chris said, 'I can't drive a car.'
   Chris said that he _____
   _____

2 'We haven't been to Prague,' she told me.
   _____
   _____

3 'I'm doing my homework,' Anna told Jack.
   _____
   _____

4 'They took the bus,' said Nick.
   _____
   _____

5 'We're going to miss the plane,' James said.
   _____
   _____

6 'There'll be a delay,' we told Harriet.
   _____
   _____

Grammar review: Units 1–9

5 **Complete the text with the words in the box.**

> are expected   could predict   is going to
> might have   riding   said   told   who
> will we   won't

In 50 years' time, what forms of road transport
(1) _____ have? Oil (2) _____ run out,
so we (3) _____ use much petrol. Cars and
buses (4) _____ electric engines. Our
researchers (5) _____ us that cycling would
increase and (6) _____ bikes doesn't use
petrol! They also (7) _____ that people
(8) _____ lived near schools and work
places would go on foot more. Electric vehicles
(9) _____ to be more common, but
will this happen? Well, if we (10) _____
the future, we'd be rich.

Revision: Units 7-9

Vocabulary

1 Complete the dialogue with the words in the box.

ambitious amusing call off come up with
confused determined developments find out
hard-working inventors research successful

Dr No So, Yuri, have there been any new
(1) _____? The radars
must be ready before the police
(2) _____ about us. I don't want
to (3) _____ our amazing
plan now. I am (4) _____ to
succeed! We will rule the world!

Yuri Don't worry. The (5) _____ say
that they have (6) _____ the
best system in the world.

Dr No Are they too (7) _____?

Yuri No, I've read their (8) _____ and
it's very good. They built the system
very quickly because they are so
(9) _____.

Dr No And our idea for the police computers?

Yuri Yes, that was (10) _____ too.

Dr No Good. Let's watch the Earth police on our
screen. Look! Their computers don't work!
The police are all (11) _____!
This is very (12) _____!

2 Complete the text with the travel words in the box.

flight tour travel trips

Enjoy a (1) _____ of the Mediterranean!
We have (2) _____ leaving three times a
week. There is a choice of (3) _____
options, including a daily (4) _____ from
Heathrow.

3 Choose the correct answer.

1 You **catch** / **take** a plane at an airport.
2 At the train station, ask for **platform** / **runway** 22.
3 Can you **drive** / **ride** a motorcycle?
4 Go to the check-in **desk** / **gate** at 17.00.
5 The train had a lot of **carriages** / **luggage**.
6 Oh, no! There's going to be a **delay** / **departure**!

4 Complete the dialogue with the travel words in
the box.

annoyed arrivals came across find out flight
journey lucky luggage resourceful travel

Mel Did you (1) _____ their
(2) _____ number?

Ben Yes, I (3) _____ all their
(4) _____ details on the computer.

Mel Good idea! You're so (5) _____!

Ben Well, I was (6) _____ actually. I
found it very easily.

Mel When do we need to be at (7) _____?

Ben Twelve thirty.

Mel Right, let's go. They've had a long
(8) _____ and they'll be
(9) _____ if we're late. They've got
a lot of (10) _____ and we need to
help them.

Grammar

1 **Rewrite the active sentences in the present simple passive.**

1   We use the computer every evening.
_____

2   Do they sell bus tickets here?
_____

3   Where do you keep the sugar?
_____

4   They do not produce Nokia phones in Spain.
_____

5   They speak English in Australia.
_____

6   We do not use our car for short journeys.
_____

7   You make kebab with meat.
_____

8   They spend millions of euros on new players.
_____
_____

2 **Write past simple passive sentences.**

1   the letter / not send / until today
_____
_____

2   this cake / cook / yesterday / ?
_____
_____

3   my hairdryer / repair / quite quickly
_____
_____

4   the internet / not invent / by an American
_____
_____

5   my homework / finish / on time
_____
_____

6   she / invite / by John's brother / ?
_____
_____

7   this book / not write / by a woman
_____
_____

8   this photo / take / in New York / ?
_____
_____

3 **Complete the sentences with the relative pronouns in the box. Then cross ✗ the two sentences where we can omit the relative pronoun.**

when   where   which   who   whose

1   That's the girl _____ father drives a taxi. ☐

2   Let's go to the park _____ they do BMXing. ☐

3   Tell me about the day _____ you missed your flight. ☐

4   Was it Mr Fruen _____ lent me this dictionary? ☐

5   That's the DVD _____ I'd like to watch. ☐

4 **Write sentences with the relative pronouns from exercise 3.**

1   Rugby is an international sport. It was invented in England.
_____
_____

2   I'm thinking of the season. We scored 53 goals!
_____
_____

3   She's the teacher. She gives hard tests.
_____
_____

4   It's a useful shop. They sell second-hand CDs.
_____
_____

5   That's the woman. Her car was stolen.
_____
_____

5 Complete the sentences with *whose* or *who's*.

1 He's the boy _____ parents own the café.
2 Let's speak to the teacher _____ organising the trip.
3 We need someone _____ a singer and a guitarist.
4 She's the coach _____ team always loses.

6 Choose the correct answer.

1 'We're thinking.'
She said that they **are thinking** / **were thinking**.
2 'They aren't at home.'
He said that they **hadn't been** / **weren't** at home.
3 'We've written to you.'
They said that they **had written** / **wrote** to us.
4 'It'll be dark at 7.00.'
She said that it **will** / **would** be dark at 7.00.
5 'Leeds won 3–0.'
He said that Leeds **had won** / **have won** 3–0.

7 Complete the sentences with *said* or *told*.

1 We _____ them that it had been a great experience.
2 Lisa _____ that she'd phone me.
3 They _____ that they were sorry.
4 Fran _____ us that it was late.

8 Report the statements.

1 'It'll rain,' she told us.
_____
_____

2 'She's made a lot of friends,' he said.
_____
_____

3 'You haven't finished,' he told her.
_____
_____

4 'It's really cool,' I said.
_____
_____

5 'They're swimming,' he told me.
_____
_____

9 Complete the text with the words in the box.

hadn't been   had waited   said   said   told   told
wasn't caught   was stolen   were called   which
who   would buy

Andy (1) _____ Becky that he loved her and that he wanted to marry her. Becky said that she (2) _____ her whole life for this moment. Andy was the man (3) _____ she had always wanted. Andy gave Becky a ring (4) _____ was beautiful – and huge.

Two weeks later, there was a robbery at their house and Becky's ring (5) _____. The police (6) _____ to the house, but the thief (7) _____.

Andy said that he (8) _____ another ring, but Becky was worried about the cost. 'Rings are very expensive,' she (9) _____.

Andy began to feel really nervous. In the end, he (10) _____ her that the ring had cost £7.99. 'I got it in the newsagent's,' he (11) _____.

Becky screamed and she said that she (12) _____ so angry in her whole life.

1 Do the culture quiz. Look for the answers in your Student's Book and Workbook if necessary.

Section A The <u>underlined</u> places are in the wrong sentences. Write the correct place for each sentence.
(1 point for each correct answer)

1 Berlin is in <u>Austria</u>. _____.

2 The Channel Tunnel connects France and <u>Germany</u>. _____

3 The anti-globalisation campaigner José Bové comes from <u>Russia</u>. _____

4 Dolly the sheep was cloned in <u>England</u>. _____

5 Arnold Schwarzenegger grew up in <u>Germany</u>. _____

6 Siberia is in eastern <u>Scotland</u>. _____

Section B Answer the questions.
(3 points for each correct answer)

1 According to the *New York Sun*, what did the astronomer John Herschel see on the Moon in 1834?
_____

2 What was invented in 1989, but started as a military project in the 1960s?
_____

3 What award did Snuppy win?
_____
_____

4 When was the computer mouse invented?
_____

5 What is Martin Halstead's nickname?
_____
_____

6 Who and where is the world's youngest mayor?
_____

7 What and where is *The Cutty Sark*?
_____

8 Who rode from London to New York, and when?
_____

Your score?   **/ 30**